PROGRAMMER'S
QUICK
REFERENCE
SERIES

I BM®
ROM
BIOS

□ □ □ □ □

RAY DUNCAN

Microsoft
PRESS®

PUBLISHED BY
Microsoft Press
A Division of Microsoft Corporation
16011 NE 36th Way, Box 97017, Redmond, Washington 98073-9717

Library of Congress Cataloging in Publication Data

Duncan, Ray, 1952-
IBM ROM BIOS.
1. IBM microcomputers—Programming.   2. Read-only storage.
I. Title.
QA76.8.I2594D84   1988   004.5'3   88-8989
ISBN 1-55615-135-7

Printed and bound in the United States of America.

1 2 3 4 5 6 7 8 9   WAKWAK   3 2 1 0 9 8

Distributed to the book trade in the United States
by Harper & Row.

Distributed to the book trade in Canada by General
Publishing Company, Ltd.

Distributed to the book trade outside the United States
and Canada by Penguin Books Ltd.

Penguin Books Ltd., Harmondsworth, Middlesex, England
Penguin Books Australia Ltd., Ringwood, Victoria, Australia
Penguin Books N.Z. Ltd., 182-190 Wairau Road, Auckland 10,
New Zealand

British Cataloging in Publication Data available

Notes to the Reader

In the Video Driver section (Int 10H), the following icons are used:

[MDA]	Monochrome Display Adapter
[CGA]	Color/Graphics Adapter
[PCjr]	PCjr system board video controller
[EGA]	Enhanced Graphics Adapter
[MCGA]	Multi-Color Graphics Array (PS/2 Models 25 and 30)
[VGA]	Video Graphics Array (PS/2 Models 50 and above)

In the remaining sections, the following icons are used:

[PC]	Original IBM PC, PC/XT, and PCjr unless otherwise noted.
[AT]	PC/AT and PC/XT-286 unless otherwise noted.
[PS/2]	All PS/2 models (including Models 25 and 30) unless otherwise noted.

ROM BIOS functions that are unique to the PC Convertible have been omitted.

There are some functions that are only supported in very late revisions of a particular machine's ROM BIOS (such as Int 1AH Functions 00H and 01H on the PC/XT). In general, such functions are not given an icon for that machine because a program could not safely assume that they were available based on the machine's ID byte(s).

Contents

Int	Function	Subfunction	Name
10H	07H		Initialize or Scroll Down Window
10H	08H		Read Character and Attribute at Cursor
10H	09H		Write Character and Attribute at Cursor
10H	0AH		Write Character at Cursor
10H	0BH		Set Palette, Background, or Border
10H	0CH		Write Graphics Pixel
10H	0DH		Read Graphics Pixel
10H	0EH		Write Character in Teletype Mode
10H	0FH		Get Video Mode
10H	10H	00H	Set Palette Register
10H	10H	01H	Set Border Color
10H	10H	02H	Set Palette and Border
10H	10H	03H	Toggle Blink/Intensity Bit
10H	10H	07H	Get Palette Register
10H	10H	08H	Get Border Color
10H	10H	09H	Get Palette and Border
10H	10H	10H	Set Color Register
10H	10H	12H	Set Block of Color Registers
10H	10H	13H	Set Color Page State
10H	10H	15H	Get Color Register
10H	10H	17H	Get Block of Color Registers
10H	10H	1AH	Get Color Page State
10H	10H	1BH	Set Gray-Scale Values
10H	11H	00H and 10H	Load User Font and Reprogram Controller
10H	11H	01H and 11H	Load ROM 8-by-14 Font and Reprogram Controller
10H	11H	02H and 12H	Load ROM 8-by-8 Font and Reprogram Controller
10H	11H	03H	Set Block Specifier
10H	11H	04H and 14H	Load ROM 8-by-16 Font and Reprogram Controller
10H	11H	20H	Set Int 1FH Font Pointer
10H	11H	21H	Set Int 43H for User's Font

(continued)

Int	Func-tion	Sub-function	Name
10H	11H	22H	Set Int 43H for ROM 8-by-14 Font
10H	11H	23H	Set Int 43H for ROM 8-by-8 Font
10H	11H	24H	Set Int 43H for ROM 8-by-16 Font
10H	11H	30H	Get Font Information
10H	12H	10H	Get Configuration Information
10H	12H	20H	Select Alternate PrintScreen
10H	12H	30H	Set Scan Lines
10H	12H	31H	Enable/Disable Default Palette Loading
10H	12H	32H	Enable/Disable Video
10H	12H	33H	Enable/Disable Gray-Scale Summing
10H	12H	34H	Enable/Disable Cursor Emulation
10H	12H	35H	Switch Active Display
10H	12H	36H	Enable/Disable Screen Refresh
10H	13H		Write String in Teletype Mode
10H	1AH		Get or Set Display Combination Code
10H	1BH		Get Functionality/State Information
10H	1CH		Save or Restore Video State
11H			Get Equipment Configuration
12H			Get Conventional Memory Size
13H			Disk Driver
13H	00H		Reset Disk System
13H	01H		Get Disk System Status
13H	02H		Read Sector
13H	03H		Write Sector
13H	04H		Verify Sector
13H	05H		Format Track
13H	06H		Format Bad Track
13H	07H		Format Drive
13H	08H		Get Drive Parameters

(continued)

Int	Func-tion	Sub-function	Name
13H	09H		Initialize Fixed Disk Characteristics
13H	0AH		Read Sector Long
13H	0BH		Write Sector Long
13H	0CH		Seek
13H	0DH		Reset Fixed Disk System
13H	0EH		Read Sector Buffer
13H	0FH		Write Sector Buffer
13H	10H		Get Drive Status
13H	11H		Recalibrate Drive
13H	12H		Controller RAM Diagnostic
13H	13H		Controller Drive Diagnostic
13H	14H		Controller Internal Diagnostic
13H	15H		Get Disk Type
13H	16H		Get Disk Change Status
13H	17H		Set Disk Type
13H	18H		Set Media Type for Format
13H	19H		Park Heads
13H	1AH		Format ESDI Drive
14H			Serial Communications Port Driver
14H	00H		Initialize Communications Port
14H	01H		Write Character to Communications Port
14H	02H		Read Character from Communications Port
14H	03H		Get Communications Port Status
14H	04H		Extended Initialize Communications Port
14H	05H		Extended Communications Port Control
15H			I/O Subsystem Extensions
15H	00H		Turn On Cassette Motor
15H	01H		Turn Off Cassette Motor
15H	02H		Read Cassette

(continued)

4

Int	Function	Sub-function	Name
15H	03H		Write Cassette
15H	0FH		Format ESDI Drive Periodic Interrupt
15H	21H	00H	Read POST Error Log
15H	21H	01H	Write POST Error Log
15H	4FH		Keyboard Intercept
15H	80H		Device Open
15H	81H		Device Close
15H	82H		Process Termination
15H	83H		Event Wait
15H	84H		Read Joystick
15H	85H		SysReq Key
15H	86H		Delay
15H	87H		Move Extended Memory Block
15H	88H		Get Extended Memory Size
15H	89H		Enter Protected Mode
15H	90H		Device Wait
15H	91H		Device Post
15H	C0H		Get System Environment
15H	C1H		Get Address of Extended BIOS Data Area
15H	C2H	00H	Enable/Disable Pointing Device
15H	C2H	01H	Reset Pointing Device
15H	C2H	02H	Set Sample Rate
15H	C2H	03H	Set Resolution
15H	C2H	04H	Get Pointing Device Type
15H	C2H	05H	Initialize Pointing Device Interface
15H	C2H	06H	Set Scaling or Get Status
15H	C2H	07H	Set Pointing Device Handler Address
15H	C3H		Set Watchdog Time-Out
15H	C4H		Programmable Option Select
16H			Keyboard Driver
16H	00H		Read Character from Keyboard
16H	01H		Get Keyboard Status

(continued)

Int	Func-tion	Sub-function	Name
16H	02H		Get Keyboard Flags
16H	03H		Set Repeat Rate
16H	04H		Set Keyclick
16H	05H		Push Character and Scan Code
16H	10H		Read Character from Enhanced Keyboard
16H	11H		Get Enhanced Keyboard Status
16H	12H		Get Enhanced Keyboard Flags
17H			Parallel Port Printer Driver
17H	00H		Write Character to Printer
17H	01H		Initialize Printer Port
17H	02H		Get Printer Status
18H			ROM BASIC
19H			Reboot System
1AH			Real-time (CMOS) Clock Driver
1AH	00H		Get Tick Count
1AH	01H		Set Tick Count
1AH	02H		Get Time
1AH	03H		Set Time
1AH	04H		Get Date
1AH	05H		Set Date
1AH	06H		Set Alarm
1AH	07H		Reset Alarm
1AH	0AH		Get Day Count
1AH	0BH		Set Day Count
1AH	80H		Set Sound Source

Interrupt Usage Table
I/O Port Usage Table
Video Attributes and Colors Table

Int 10H Function 00H
Set Video Mode

[MDA] [CGA] [PCjr]
[EGA] [MCGA] [VGA]

Selects the current video display mode. Also selects the active video controller, if more than one is present.

Call with:

AH	= 00H
AL	= video mode (see Notes)

Returns:

Nothing

Notes:

■ The video modes applicable to the various IBM machine models and video adapters are as follows:

Mode	Resolution	Colors	Text/ Graphics	MDA	CGA	PCjr	EGA	MCGA	VGA
00H	40-by-25 color burst off	16	text		■	■	■	■	■
01H	40-by-25	16	text		■	■	■	■	■
02H	80-by-25 color burst off	16	text		■	■	■	■	■
03H	80-by-25	16	text		■	■	■	■	■
04H	320-by-200	4	graphics		■	■	■	■	■
05H	320-by-200 color burst off	4	graphics		■	■	■	■	■
06H	640-by-200	2	graphics		■	■	■	■	■
07H	80-by-25	2*	text	■			■		■
08H	160-by-200	16	graphics			■			
09H	320-by-200	16	graphics			■			
0AH	640-by-200	4	graphics			■			
0BH	reserved								
0CH	reserved								

*Monochrome monitor only.

(continued)

Mode	Resolution	Colors	Text/ Graphics	MDA	CGA	PCjr	EGA	MCGA	VGA
0DH	320-by-200	16	graphics				■		■
0EH	640-by-200	16	graphics				■		■
0FH	640-by-350	2*	graphics				■		■
10H	640-by-350	4	graphics				■†		
10H	640-by-350	16	graphics				■‡		■
11H	640-by-480	2	graphics					■	■
12H	640-by-480	16	graphics						■
13H	320-by-200	256	graphics					■	■

*Monochrome monitor only.
†EGA with 64 KB of RAM.
‡EGA with 128 KB or more of RAM.

■ The presence or absence of color burst is only significant when a composite monitor is being used. For RGB monitors, there is no functional difference between modes 00H and 01H or modes 02H and 03H. On the CGA, two palettes are available in mode 04H and one in mode 05H.

■ On the PC/AT, PCjr, and PS/2, if bit 7 of AL is set, the display buffer is not cleared when a new mode is selected. On the PC or PC/XT, this capability is available only when an EGA (which has its own ROM BIOS) is installed.

Int 10H Function 01H   [MDA] [CGA] [PCjr]
Set Cursor Type   [EGA] [MCGA] [VGA]

Selects the starting and ending lines for the blinking hardware cursor in text display modes.

Call with:

AH	= 01H
CH bits 0–4	= starting line for cursor
CL bits 0–4	= ending line for cursor

Returns:

Nothing

Notes:

- In text display modes, the video hardware causes the cursor to blink, and the blink cannot be disabled. In graphics modes, the hardware cursor is not available.

- The default values set by the ROM BIOS are:

Display	Start	End
monochrome mode 07H	11	12
text modes 00H–03H	6	7

- On the EGA, MCGA, and VGA in text modes 00H–03H, the ROM BIOS accepts cursor start and end values as though the character cell were 8-by-8, and remaps the values as appropriate for the true character cell dimensions. This mapping is called cursor emulation.

- You can turn off the cursor in several ways. On the MDA, CGA, and VGA, setting register CH = 20H causes the cursor to disappear. Techniques that involve setting illegal starting and ending lines for the current display mode tend to be unreliable. An alternative method is to position the cursor to a nondisplayable address, such as $(x,y)=(0,25)$.

Int 10H Function 02H   [MDA] [CGA] [PCjr]
Set Cursor Position   [EGA] [MCGA] [VGA]

Positions the cursor on the display, using text coordinates.

Call with:

AH	= 02H
BH	= page
DH	= row (*y* coordinate)
DL	= column (*x* coordinate)

Returns:

Nothing

Notes:

- A separate cursor is maintained for each display page, and each can be set independently with this function regardless of the currently active page. The number of available display pages depends on the video adapter and current display mode. See Int 10H Function 05H.

- Text coordinates $(x,y)=(0,0)$ are the upper left corner of the screen.
- The maximum value for each text coordinate depends on the video adapter and current display mode, as follows:

Mode	Maximum x	Maximum y
00H	39	24
01H	39	24
02H	79	24
03H	79	24
04H	39	24
05H	39	24
06H	79	24
07H	79	24
08H	19	24
09H	39	24
0AH	79	24
0BH	reserved	
0CH	reserved	
0DH	39	24
0EH	79	24
0FH	79	24
10H	79	24
11H	79	29
12H	79	29
13H	39	24

Int 10H Function 03H   [MDA] [CGA] [PCjr]
Get Cursor Position   [EGA] [MCGA] [VGA]

Obtains the current position of the cursor on the display, in text coordinates.

Call with:

AH	= 03H
BH	= page

Returns:

CH	= starting line for cursor
CL	= ending line for cursor
DH	= row (*y* coordinate)
DL	= column (*x* coordinate)

Note:

■ A separate cursor is maintained for each display page, and each can be inspected independently with this function regardless of the currently active page. The number of available display pages depends on the video adapter and current display mode. See Int 10H Function 05H.

Int 10H Function 04H   [CGA] [PCjr] [EGA]
Get Light Pen Position

Obtains the current status and position of the light pen.

Call with:

AH	= 04H

Returns:

AH	= 00H	if light pen not down/not triggered
	01H	if light pen down/triggered
BX	= pixel column (graphics *x* coordinate)	
CH	= pixel row (graphics *y* coordinate, modes 04H–06H)	
CX	= pixel row (graphics *y* coordinate, modes 0DH–10H)	
DH	= character row (text *y* coordinate)	
DL	= character column (text *x* coordinate)	

Notes:

■ The range of text and graphics coordinates returned by this function depends on the current display mode.

■ On the CGA, the graphics coordinates returned by this function are not continuous. The *y* coordinate is always a multiple of two; the *x* coordinate is either a multiple of four (for 320-by-200 graphics modes) or a multiple of eight (for 640-by-200 graphics modes).

■ Careful selection of background and foreground colors is necessary to obtain maximum sensitivity from the light pen across the full screen width.

Int 10H Function 05H
Set Display Page

[CGA] [PCjr] [EGA]
[MCGA] [VGA]

Selects the active display page for the video display.

Call with:

For CGA, EGA, MCGA, VGA
AH = 05H
AL = page
　　　0–7　for modes 00H and 01H (CGA, EGA, MCGA, VGA)
　　　0–3　for modes 02H and 03H (CGA)
　　　0–7　for modes 02H and 03H (EGA, MCGA, VGA)
　　　0–7　for mode 07H (EGA, VGA)
　　　0–7　for mode 0DH (EGA, VGA)
　　　0–3　for mode 0EH (EGA, VGA)
　　　0–1　for mode 0FH (EGA, VGA)
　　　0–1　for mode 10H (EGA, VGA)

For PCjr only
AH = 05H
AL = subfunction
　　　80H = read CRT/CPU page registers
　　　81H = set CPU page register
　　　82H = set CRT page register
　　　83H = set both CPU and CRT page registers
BH = CRT page (Subfunctions 82H and 83H)
BL = CPU page (Subfunctions 81H and 83H)

Returns:

If CGA, EGA, MCGA, or VGA adapter
Nothing

If PCjr and if function called with AL = 80H–83H
BH = CRT page register
BL = CPU page register

Notes:

- Video mode and adapter combinations not listed above support one display page (for example, a Monochrome Adapter in mode 7).

- Switching between pages does not affect their contents. In addition, text can be written to any video page with Int 10H Functions 02H, 09H, and 0AH, regardless of the page currently being displayed.

- On the PCjr, the CPU page determines the part of the physical memory region 00000H–1FFFFH that will be hardware mapped onto 16 KB of memory beginning at segment B800H. The CRT page determines the starting address of the physical memory used by the video controller to refresh the display. Smooth animation effects can be achieved by manipulation of these registers. Programs that write directly to the B800H segment can reach only the first 16 KB of the video-refresh buffer. Programs requiring direct access to the entire 32 KB buffer in modes 09H and 0AH can obtain the current CRT page from the ROM BIOS variable PAGDAT at 0040:008AH.

Int 10H Function 06H Initialize or Scroll Up Window

[MDA] [CGA] [PCjr]
[EGA] [MCGA] [VGA]

Initializes a specified window of the display to ASCII blank characters with a given attribute, or scrolls up the contents of a window by a specified number of lines.

Call with:

AH	= 06H
AL	= number of lines to scroll (if zero, entire window is blanked)
BH	= attribute to be used for blanked area
CH	= y coordinate, upper left corner of window
CL	= x coordinate, upper left corner of window
DH	= y coordinate, lower right corner of window
DL	= x coordinate, lower right corner of window

Returns:

Nothing

Notes:

- In video modes that support multiple pages, this function affects only the page currently being displayed.
- If AL contains a value other than 00H, the area within the specified window is scrolled up by the requested number of lines. Text that is scrolled beyond the top of the window is lost. The new lines that appear at the bottom of the window are filled with ASCII blanks carrying the attribute specified by register BH.

- To scroll down the contents of a window, see Int 10H Function 07H.

Int 10H Function 07H
Initialize or
Scroll Down Window

[MDA] [CGA] [PCjr]
[EGA] [MCGA] [VGA]

Initializes a specified window of the display to ASCII blank characters with a given attribute, or scrolls down the contents of a window by a specified number of lines.

Call with:

AH	= 07H
AL	= number of lines to scroll (if zero, entire window is blanked)
BH	= attribute to be used for blanked area
CH	= y coordinate, upper left corner of window
CL	= x coordinate, upper left corner of window
DH	= y coordinate, lower right corner of window
DL	= x coordinate, lower right corner of window

Returns:

Nothing

Notes:

- In video modes that support multiple pages, this function affects only the page currently being displayed.

- If AL contains a value other than 00H, the area within the specified window is scrolled down by the requested number of lines. Text that is scrolled beyond the bottom of the window is lost. The new lines that appear at the top of the window are filled with ASCII blanks carrying the attribute specified by register BH.

- To scroll up the contents of a window, see Int 10H Function 06H.

Int 10H Function 08H
Read Character and
Attribute at Cursor

[MDA] [CGA] [PCjr]
[EGA] [MCGA] [VGA]

Obtains the ASCII character and its attribute at the current cursor position for the specified display page.

Call with:

AH	= 08H
BH	= page

Returns:

AH	= attribute
AL	= character

Note:

■ In video modes that support multiple pages, characters and their attributes can be read from any page, regardless of the page currently being displayed.

Int 10H Function 09H
Write Character and
Attribute at Cursor

[MDA] [CGA] [PCjr]
[EGA] [MCGA] [VGA]

Writes an ASCII character and its attribute to the display at the current cursor position.

Call with:

AH	= 09H
AL	= character
BH	= page
BL	= attribute (text modes) or color (graphics modes)
CX	= count of characters to write (replication factor)

Returns:

Nothing

Notes:

- In graphics modes, the replication factor in CX produces a valid result only for the current row. If more characters are written than there are remaining columns in the current row, the result is unpredictable.

- All values of AL result in some sort of display; control characters, including bell, backspace, carriage return, and line feed, are not recognized as special characters and do not affect the cursor position.

- After a character is written, the cursor must be moved explicitly with Int 10H Function 02H to the next position.

- To write a character without changing the attribute at the current cursor position, use Int 10H Function 0AH.

- If this function is used to write characters in graphics mode and bit 7 of BL is set (1), the character will be exclusive-OR'd (XOR) with the current display contents. This feature can be used to write characters and then "erase" them.

- For the CGA and PCjr in graphics modes 04H–06H, the bit patterns for character codes 80H–FFH are obtained from a table whose address is stored in the vector for Int 1FH. On the PCjr, the address of the table for character codes 00–7FH is stored in the vector for Int 44H. Alternative character sets can be installed by loading them into memory and updating this vector.

- For the EGA, MCGA, and VGA in graphics modes, the address of the character definition table is stored in the vector for Int 43H. See Int 10H Function 11H.

Int 10H Function 0AH   [MDA] [CGA] [PCjr]
Write Character   [EGA] [MCGA] [VGA]
at Cursor

Writes an ASCII character to the display at the current cursor position. The character receives the attribute of the previous character displayed at the same position.

Call with:

AH	= 0AH
AL	= character
BH	= page

| BL | = color (graphics modes, PCjr only) |
| CX | = count of characters to write (replication factor) |

Returns:

Nothing

Notes:

■ In graphics modes, the replication factor in CX produces a valid result only for the current row. If more characters are written than there are remaining columns in the current row, the result is unpredictable.

■ All values of AL result in some sort of display; control characters, including bell, backspace, carriage return, and line feed, are not recognized as special characters and do not affect the cursor position.

■ After a character is written, the cursor must be moved explicitly with Int 10H Function 02H to the next position.

■ To write a character and attribute at the current cursor position, use Int 10H Function 09H.

■ If this function is used to write characters in graphics mode and bit 7 of BL is set (1), the character will be exclusive-OR'd (XOR) with the current display contents. This feature can be used to write characters and then "erase" them.

■ For the CGA and PCjr in graphics modes 04H–06H, the bit patterns for character codes 80H–FFH are obtained from a table whose address is stored in the vector for Int 1FH. On the PCjr, the address of the table for character codes 00–7FH is stored in the vector for Int 44H. Alternative character sets can be installed by loading them into memory and updating this vector.

■ For the EGA, MCGA, and VGA in graphics modes, the address of the character definition table is stored in the vector for Int 43H. See Int 10H Function 11H.

Int 10H Function 0BH
Set Palette, Background,
or Border

[CGA] [PCjr] [EGA]
[MCGA] [VGA]

Selects a palette, background, or border color.

Call with:

To set the background color and border color for graphics modes or the border color for text modes

AH = 0BH
BH = 00H
BL = color

To select the palette (320-by-200 4-color graphics modes)

AH = 0BH
BH = 01H
BL = palette (see Notes)

Returns:

Nothing

Notes:

■ In text modes, this function selects only the border color. The background color of each individual character is controlled by the upper 4 bits of that character's attribute byte.

■ On the CGA and EGA, this function is valid for palette selection only in 320-by-200 4-color graphics modes.

■ In 320-by-200 4-color graphics modes, if register BH = 01H, the following palettes may be selected:

Palette	Pixel value	Color
0	0	same as background
	1	green
	2	red
	3	brown or yellow
1	0	same as background
	1	cyan
	2	magenta
	3	white

■ On the CGA in 640-by-200 2-color graphics mode, the background color selected with this function actually controls the display color for nonzero pixels; zero pixels are always displayed as black.

■ On the PCjr in 640-by-200 2-color graphics mode, if BH = 00H and bit 0 of register BL is cleared, pixel value 1 is displayed as white; if bit 0 is set, pixel value 1 is displayed as black.

■ See also Int 10H Function 10H, which is used for palette programming on the PCjr, EGA, MCGA, and VGA.

Int 10H Function 0CH
Write Graphics Pixel

Draws a point on the display at the specified graphics coordinates.

Call with:

AH	= 0CH
AL	= pixel value
BH	= page
CX	= column (graphics *x* coordinate)
DX	= row (graphics *y* coordinate)

Returns:

Nothing

Notes:

- The range of valid pixel values and (*x,y*) coordinates depends on the current video mode.

- If bit 7 of AL is set, the new pixel value will be exclusive-OR'd (XOR) with the current contents of the pixel.

- Register BH is ignored for display modes that support only one page.

Int 10H Function 0DH
Read Graphics Pixel

Obtains the current value of the pixel on the display at the specified graphics coordinates.

Call with:

AH	= 0DH
BH	= page
CX	= column (graphics *x* coordinate)
DX	= row (graphics *y* coordinate)

Returns:

AL	= pixel value

Notes:

- The range of valid (x,y) coordinates and possible pixel values depends on the current video mode.

- Register BH is ignored for display modes that support only one page.

Int 10H Function 0EH
Write Character in
Teletype Mode

[MDA] [CGA] [PCjr]
[EGA] [MCGA] [VGA]

Writes an ASCII character to the display at the current cursor position, using the specified color (if in graphics modes), and then increments the cursor position appropriately.

Call with:

AH	= 0EH
AL	= character
BH	= page
BL	= foreground color (graphics modes)

Returns:

Nothing

Notes:

- The special ASCII codes for bell (07H), backspace (08H), carriage return (0DH), and line feed (0AH) are recognized, and the appropriate action is taken. All other characters are written to the display (even if they are control characters), and the cursor is moved to the next position.

- In video modes that support multiple pages, characters can be written to any page, regardless of the page currently being displayed.

- Line wrapping and scrolling are provided. If the cursor is at the end of a line, it is moved to the beginning of the next line. If the cursor reaches the end of the last line on the screen, the screen is scrolled up by one line and the cursor is placed at the beginning of a new blank line. The attribute for the entire new line is taken from the last character that was written on the preceding line.

- The default MS-DOS console driver (CON) uses this function to write text to the screen. You cannot use this function to specify the attribute of a character. One method of writing a character to the screen with a specific attribute is to first write an ASCII blank (20H) with the desired attribute at the current cursor location using Int 10H Function 09H, then write the actual character with Int 10H Function 0EH. This technique, although somewhat clumsy, does not require the program to explicitly handle line wrapping and scrolling.
- See also Int 10H Function 13H.

Int 10H Function 0FH   [MDA] [CGA] [PCjr]
Get Video Mode   [EGA] [MCGA] [VGA]

Obtains the current display mode of the active video controller.

Call with:

AH   = 0FH

Returns:

AH   = number of character columns on screen
AL   = display mode (see Int 10H Function 00H)
BH   = active display page

Note:

- This function can be called to obtain the screen width before clearing the screen with Int 10H Functions 06H or 07H.

Int 10H Function 10H   [PCjr] [EGA]
Subfunction 00H   [MCGA] [VGA]
Set Palette Register

Sets the correspondence of a palette register to a displayable color.

Call with:

For PCjr, EGA, or VGA
AH   = 10H
AL   = 00H
BH   = color value
BL   = palette register (00–0FH)

For MCGA

AH	= 10H
AL	= 00H
BX	= 0712H

Returns:

Nothing

Note:

■ On the MCGA, this function can only be called with BX = 0712H and selects a color register set with eight consistent colors.

Int 10H Function 10H   [PCjr] [EGA] [VGA]
Subfunction 01H
Set Border Color

Controls the color of the screen border (overscan).

Call with:

AH	= 10H
AL	= 01H
BH	= color value

Returns:

Nothing

Int 10H Function 10H   [PCjr] [EGA] [VGA]
Subfunction 02H
Set Palette and Border

Sets all palette registers and the border color (overscan) in one operation.

Call with:

AH	= 10H
AL	= 02H
ES:DX	= segment:offset of color list

Returns:

Nothing

Notes:

- The color list is 17 bytes long. The first 16 bytes are the color values to be loaded into palette registers 0–15, and the last byte is stored in the border color register.

- In 16-color graphics modes, the following default palette is set up:

Pixel value	Color
01H	blue
02H	green
03H	cyan
04H	red
05H	magenta
06H	brown
07H	white
08H	gray
09H	light blue
0AH	light green
0BH	light cyan
0CH	light red
0DH	light magenta
0EH	yellow
0FH	intense white

Int 10H Function 10H
Subfunction 03H
Toggle Blink/Intensity Bit

[PCjr] [EGA]
[MCGA] [VGA]

Determines whether the most significant bit of a character attribute will select blinking or intensified display.

Call with:

AH	= 10H
AL	= 03H
BL	= blink/intensity toggle
	0 = enable intensity
	1 = enable blinking

Int 10H Function 10H
Subfunction 07H
Get Palette Register

[VGA]

Returns the color associated with the specified palette register.

Call with:

AH	= 10H
AL	= 07H
BL	= palette register

Returns:

BH	= color

Int 10H Function 10H
Subfunction 08H
Get Border Color

[VGA]

Returns the current border color (overscan).

Call with:

AH	= 10H
AL	= 08H

Returns:

BH	= color

Int 10H Function 10H
Subfunction 09H
Get Palette and Border

[VGA]

Gets the contents of all palette registers and the border color (over-scan) in one operation.

Call with:

AH	= 10H
AL	= 09H
ES:DX	= segment:offset of 17-byte buffer

Returns:

ES:DX	= segment:offset of buffer

and buffer contains palette values in bytes 00H–0FH and border color in byte 10H.

Int 10H Function 10H [MCGA] [VGA]
Subfunction 10H
Set Color Register

Programs an individual color register with a red-green-blue (RGB) combination.

Call with:

AH	= 10H
AL	= 10H
BX	= color register
CH	= green value
CL	= blue value
DH	= red value

Returns:

Nothing

Note:

■ If gray-scale summing is enabled, the weighted gray-scale value is calculated as described under Int 10H Function 10H Subfunction 1BH and is stored into all three components of the color register. See also Int 10H Function 12H Subfunction 33H.

Int 10H Function 10H
Subfunction 12H
Set Block of Color Registers

[MCGA] [VGA]

Programs a group of consecutive color registers in one operation.

Call with:

AH	= 10H
AL	= 12H
BX	= first color register
CX	= number of color registers
ES:DX	= segment:offset of color table

Returns:

Nothing

Notes:

- The table consists of a series of 3-byte entries, one entry per color register to be programmed. The bytes of an individual entry specify the red, green, and blue values (in that order) for the associated color register.

- If gray-scale summing is enabled, the weighted gray-scale value for each register is calculated as described under Int 10H Function 10H Subfunction 1BH and is stored into all three components of the color register. See also Int 10H Function 12H Subfunction 33H.

Int 10H Function 10H
Subfunction 13H
Set Color Page State

[VGA]

Selects the paging mode for the color registers, or selects an individual page of color registers.

Call with:

To select the paging mode

AH	= 10H
AL	= 13H
BH	= paging mode

	00H	*for 4 pages of 64 registers*
	01H	*for 16 pages of 16 registers*
BL	= 00H	

To select a color register page

AH	= 10H
AL	= 13H
BH	= page
BL	= 01H

Returns:

Nothing

Note:

■ This function is not valid in mode 13H (320-by-200 256-color graphics).

Int 10H Function 10H Subfunction 15H Get Color Register

[MCGA] [VGA]

Returns the contents of a color register as its red, green, and blue components.

Call with:

AH	= 10H
AL	= 15H
BX	= color register

Returns:

CH	= green value
CL	= blue value
DH	= red value

Int 10H Function 10H Subfunction 17H Get Block of Color Registers

[MCGA] [VGA]

Allows the red, green, and blue components associated with each of a set of color registers to be read in one operation.

Call with:

AH	= 10H
AL	= 17H
BX	= first color register
CX	= number of color registers
ES:DX	= segment:offset of buffer to receive color list

Returns:

ES:DX	= segment:offset of buffer

and buffer contains color list

Note:

■ The color list returned in the caller's buffer consists of a series of 3-byte entries corresponding to the color registers. Each 3-byte entry contains the register's red, green, and blue components in that order.

Int 10H Function 10H   [VGA]
Subfunction 1AH
Get Color Page State

Returns the color register paging mode and current color page.

Call with:

AH	= 10H
AL	= 1AH

Returns:

BH	= color page
BL	= paging mode
	00H if 4 pages of 64 registers
	01H if 16 pages of 16 registers

Note:

■ See Int 10H Function 10H Subfunction 13H, which allows selection of the paging mode or current color page.

Int 10H Function 10H [MCGA] [VGA]
Subfunction 1BH
Set Gray-Scale Values

Transforms the red, green, and blue values of one or more color registers into the gray-scale equivalents.

Call with:

AH	= 10H
AL	= 1BH
BX	= first color register
CX	= number of color registers

Returns:

Nothing

Note:

- For each color register, the weighted sum of its red, green, and blue values is calculated (30% red + 59% green + 11% blue) and written back into all three components of the color register. The original red, green, and blue values are lost.

Int 10H Function 11H [EGA] [MCGA] [VGA]
Subfunctions 00H and 10H
Load User Font and
Reprogram Controller

Loads the user's font (character definition) table into the specified block of character generator RAM.

Call with:

AH	= 11H
AL	= 00H or 10H (see Notes)
BH	= points (bytes per character)
BL	= block
CX	= number of characters defined by table
DX	= first character code in table
ES:BP	= segment:offset of font table

Returns:

Nothing

Notes:

■ This function provides font selection in text (alphanumeric) display modes. For font selection in graphics (all-points-addressable) modes, see Int 10H Function 11H Subfunctions 20H–24H.

■ If AL = 10H, page 0 must be active. The points (bytes per character), rows, and length of the refresh buffer are recalculated. The controller is reprogrammed with the maximum scan line ($points - 1$), cursor start ($points - 2$), cursor end ($points - 1$), vertical display end (($rows*points$) $- 1$), and underline location ($points - 1$, mode 7 only).

If Subfunction 10H is called at any time other than immediately after a mode set, the results are unpredictable.

■ On the MCGA, a Subfunction 00H call should be followed by a Subfunction 03H call so that the ROM BIOS will load the font into the character generator's internal font pages.

■ Subfunction 10H is reserved on the MCGA. If it is called, Subfunction 00H is executed.

Int 10H Function 11H   [EGA] [VGA]
Subfunctions 01H and 11H
Load ROM 8-by-14 Font and
Reprogram Controller

Loads the ROM BIOS default 8-by-14 font table into the specified block of character generator RAM.

Call with:

AH	= 11H
AL	= 01H or 11H (see Notes)
BL	= block

Returns:

Nothing

Notes:

■ This function provides font selection in text (alphanumeric) display modes. For font selection in graphics (all-points-addressable) modes, see Int 10H Function 11H Subfunctions 20H–24H.

- If AL = 11H, page 0 must be active. The points (bytes per character), rows, and length of the refresh buffer are recalculated. The controller is reprogrammed with the maximum scan line (*points* − *1*), cursor start (*points* − *2*), cursor end (*points* − *1*), vertical display end ((*rows*points*) − *1*), and underline location (*points* − *1*, mode 7 only).

  If Subfunction 11H is called at any time other than immediately after a mode set, the results are unpredictable.

- Subfunctions 01H and 11H are reserved on the MCGA. If either is called, Subfunction 04H is executed.

Int 10H Function 11H   [EGA] [MCGA] [VGA]
Subfunctions 02H and 12H
Load ROM 8-by-8 Font and
Reprogram Controller

Loads the ROM BIOS default 8-by-8 font table into the specified block of character generator RAM.

Call with:

AH	= 11H
AL	= 02H or 12H (see Notes)
BL	= block

Returns:

Nothing

Notes:

- This function provides font selection in text (alphanumeric) display modes. For font selection in graphics (all-points-addressable) modes, see Int 10H Function 11H Subfunctions 20H–24H.

- If AL = 12H, page 0 must be active. The points (bytes per character), rows, and length of the refresh buffer are recalculated. The controller is reprogrammed with the maximum scan line (*points* − *1*), cursor start (*points* − *2*), cursor end (*points* − *1*), vertical display end ((*rows*points*) − *1*), and underline location (*points* − *1*, mode 7 only).

  If Subfunction 12H is called at any time other than immediately after a mode set, the results are unpredictable.

- On the MCGA, a Subfunction 02H call should be followed by a Subfunction 03H call, so that the ROM BIOS will load the font into the character generator's internal font pages.

- Subfunction 12H is reserved on the MCGA. If it is called, Subfunction 02H is executed.

Int 10H Function 11H   [EGA] [MCGA] [VGA]
Subfunction 03H
Set Block Specifier

Determines the character blocks selected by bit 3 of character attribute bytes in alphanumeric (text) display modes.

Call with:

AH	= 11H
AL	= 03H
BL	= character generator block select code (see Notes)

Returns:

Nothing

Notes:

- On the EGA and MCGA, the bits of BL are used as follows:

Bits	*Significance*
0–1	character block selected by attribute bytes with bit 3 = 0
2–3	character block selected by attribute bytes with bit 3 = 1
4–7	not used (should be 0)

- On the VGA, the bits of BL are used as follows:

Bits	*Significance*
0,1,4	character block selected by attribute bytes with bit 3 = 0
2,3,5	character block selected by attribute bytes with bit 3 = 1
6–7	not used (should be 0)

- When using a 256-character set, both fields of BL should select the same character block. In such cases, character attribute bit 3 controls the foreground intensity. When using 512-character sets, the fields of BL designate the blocks holding each half of the character set, and bit 3 of the character attribute selects the upper or lower half of the character set.

- When using a 512-character set, a call to Int 10H Function 10H Subfunction 00H with BX = 0712H is recommended to set the color planes to eight consistent colors.

Int 10H Function 11H [MCGA] [VGA]
Subfunctions 04H and 14H
Load ROM 8-by-16 Font and
Reprogram Controller

Loads the ROM BIOS default 8-by-16 font table into the specified block of character generator RAM.

Call with:

AH	= 11H
AL	= 04H or 14H (see Notes)
BL	= block

Returns:

Nothing

Notes:

- This function provides font selection in text (alphanumeric) display modes. For font selection in graphics (all-points-addressable) modes, see Int 10H Function 11H Subfunctions 20H–24H.

- If AL = 14H, page 0 must be active. The points (bytes per character), rows, and length of the refresh buffer are recalculated. The controller is reprogrammed with the maximum scan line (*points* − *1*), cursor start (*points* − *2*), cursor end (*points* − *1*), vertical display end (*rows*points* − *1* for 350 and 400 line modes, or *rows*points*2* − *1* for 200 line modes), and underline location (*points* − *1*, mode 7 only).

  If Subfunction 14H is called at any time other than immediately after a mode set, the results are unpredictable.

- On the MCGA, a Subfunction 04H call should be followed by a Subfunction 03H call so that the ROM BIOS will load the font into the character generator's internal font pages.

- Subfunction 14H is reserved on the MCGA. If it is called, Subfunction 04H is executed.

Int 10H Function 11H [EGA] [MCGA] [VGA]
Subfunction 20H
Set Int 1FH Font Pointer

Sets the Int 1FH pointer to the user's font table. This table is used for character codes 80H–FFH in graphics modes 04H–06H.

Call with:

AH	= 11H
AL	= 20H
ES:BP	= segment:offset of font table

Returns:

Nothing

Notes:

■ This function provides font selection in graphics (all-points-addressable) display modes. For font selection in text (alphanumeric) modes, see Int 10H Function 11H Subfunctions 00H–14H.

■ If this subfunction is called at any time other than immediately after a mode set, the results are unpredictable.

Int 10H Function 11H [EGA] [MCGA] [VGA]
Subfunction 21H
Set Int 43H for User's Font

Sets the vector for Int 43H to point to the user's font table and updates the video ROM BIOS data area. The video controller is not reprogrammed.

Call with:

AH	= 11H
AL	= 21H
BL	= character rows specifier
	00H if user specified (see register DL)
	01H = 14 (0EH) rows
	02H = 25 (19H) rows
	03H = 43 (2BH) rows

CX	= points (bytes per character)
DL	= character rows per screen (if BL = 00H)
ES:BP	= segment:offset of user font table

Returns:

Nothing

Notes:

- This function provides font selection in graphics (all-points-addressable) display modes. For font selection in text (alphanumeric) modes, see Int 10H Function 11H Subfunctions 00H–14H.

- If this subfunction is called at any time other than immediately after a mode set, the results are unpredictable.

Int 10H Function 11H [EGA] [MCGA] [VGA]
Subfunction 22H
Set Int 43H for ROM 8-by-14 Font

Sets the vector for Int 43H to point to the ROM BIOS default 8-by-14 font and updates the video ROM BIOS data area. The video controller is not reprogrammed.

Call with:

AH	= 11H
AL	= 22H
BL	= character rows specifier
	00H if user specified (see register DL)
	01H = 14 (0EH) rows
	02H = 25 (19H) rows
	03H = 43 (2BH) rows
DL	= character rows per screen (if BL = 00H)

Returns:

Nothing

Notes:

- This function provides font selection in graphics (all-points-addressable) display modes. For font selection in text (alphanumeric) modes, see Int 10H Function 11H Subfunctions 00H–14H.

- If this subfunction is called at any time other than immediately after a mode set, the results are unpredictable.

- When this subfunction is called on the MCGA, Subfunction 24H is substituted.

Int 10H Function 11H [EGA] [MCGA] [VGA]
Subfunction 23H
Set Int 43H for ROM 8-by-8 Font

Sets the vector for Int 43H to point to the ROM BIOS default 8-by-8 font and updates the video ROM BIOS data area. The video controller is not reprogrammed.

Call with:

AH	= 11H
AL	= 23H
BL	= character rows specifier
	00H if user specified (see register DL)
	01H = 14 (0EH) rows
	02H = 25 (19H) rows
	03H = 43 (2BH) rows
DL	= character rows per screen (if BL = 00H)

Returns:

Nothing

Notes:

- This function provides font selection in graphics (all-points-addressable) display modes. For font selection in text (alphanumeric) modes, see Int 10H Function 11H Subfunctions 00H–14H.

- If this subfunction is called at any time other than immediately after a mode set, the results are unpredictable.

Int 10H Function 11H [MCGA] [VGA]
Subfunction 24H
Set Int 43H for ROM 8-by-16 Font

Sets the vector for Int 43H to point to the ROM BIOS default 8-by-16 font and updates the video ROM BIOS data area. The video controller is not reprogrammed.

Call with:

AH	= 11H
AL	= 24H
BL	= row specifier
	00H if user specified (see register DL)
	01H = 14 (0EH) rows
	02H = 25 (19H) rows
	03H = 43 (2BH) rows
DL	= character rows per screen (if BL = 00H)

Returns:

Nothing

Notes:

- This function provides font selection in graphics (all-points-addressable) display modes. For font selection in text (alphanumeric) modes, see Int 10H Function 11H Subfunctions 00H–14H.

- If this subfunction is called at any time other than immediately after a mode set, the results are unpredictable.

Int 10H Function 11H [EGA] [MCGA] [VGA]
Subfunction 30H
Get Font Information

Returns a pointer to the character definition table for a font, and the points (bytes per character) and rows for that font.

Call with:

AH	= 11H
AL	= 30H

BH   = font code
               00H = current Int 1FH contents
               01H = current Int 43H contents
               02H = ROM 8-by-14 font (EGA, VGA only)
               03H = ROM 8-by-8 font (characters 00H–7FH)
               04H = ROM 8-by-8 font (characters 80H–FFH)
               *05H = ROM alternate 9-by-14 font (EGA, VGA
                      only)*
               06H = ROM 8-by-16 font (MCGA, VGA only)
               07H = ROM alternate 9-by-16 font (VGA only)

Returns:

CX   = points (bytes per character)
DL   = rows (character rows on screen − 1)
ES:BP   = segment:offset of font table

Int 10H Function 12H   [EGA] [VGA]
Subfunction 10H
Get Configuration Information

Obtains configuration information for the active video subsystem.

Call with:

AH   = 12H
BL   = 10H

Returns:

BH   = display type
               0H   if color display
               1H   if monochrome display
BL   = memory installed on EGA board
               00H if 64 KB
               01H if 128 KB
               02H if 192 KB
               03H if 256 KB
CH   = feature bits (see Notes)
CL   = switch setting (see Notes)

Notes:

■ The feature bits are set from Input Status register 0 in response to
  an output on the specified Feature Control register bits:

Feature Bit(s)	Feature Control Output Bit	Input Status Bit
0	0	5
1	0	6
2	1	5
3	1	6
4–7	not used	

- The bits in the switch settings byte indicate the state of the EGA's configuration DIP switch (1 = off, 0 = on).

Bit	Significance
0	configuration switch 1
1	configuration switch 2
2	configuration switch 3
3	configuration switch 4
4–7	not used

Int 10H Function 12H   [EGA] [VGA]
Subfunction 20H
Select Alternate PrintScreen

Selects an alternate print-screen routine for the EGA and VGA that works properly if the screen length is not 25 lines. The ROM BIOS default print-screen routine always prints 25 lines.

Call with:

    AH   = 12H
    BL   = 20H

Returns:

Nothing

Int 10H Function 12H [VGA]
Subfunction 30H
Set Scan Lines

Selects the number of scan lines for alphanumeric modes. The selected value takes effect the next time Int 10H Function 00H is called to select the display mode.

Call with:

AH	= 12H
AL	= scan line code
	00H = 200 scan lines
	01H = 350 scan lines
	02H = 400 scan lines
BL	= 30H

Returns:

If the VGA is active
AL   = 12H

If the VGA is not active
AL   = 00H

Int 10H Function 12H [MCGA] [VGA]
Subfunction 31H
Enable/Disable Default Palette Loading

Enables or disables loading of a default palette when a video display mode is selected.

Call with:

AH	= 12H
AL	= 00H to enable default palette loading
	01H to disable default palette loading
BL	= 31H

Returns:

If function supported
AL   = 12H

Int 10H Function 12H [MCGA] [VGA]
Subfunction 32H
Enable/Disable Video

Enables or disables CPU access to the video adapter's I/O ports and
video refresh buffer.

Call with:

AH	= 12H
AL	= 00H to enable access
	01H to disable access
BL	= 32H

Returns:

If function supported
AL   = 12H

Int 10H Function 12H [MCGA] [VGA]
Subfunction 33H
Enable/Disable Gray-Scale Summing

Enables or disables gray-scale summing for the currently active
display.

Call with:

AH	= 12H
AL	= 00H to enable gray-scale summing
	01H to disable gray-scale summing
BL	= 33H

Returns:

If function supported
AL   = 12H

Note:

■ When enabled, gray-scale summing occurs during display mode
selection, palette programming, and color register loading.

Int 10H Function 12H [VGA]
Subfunction 34H
Enable/Disable Cursor Emulation

Enables or disables cursor emulation for the currently active display.
When cursor emulation is enabled, the ROM BIOS automatically
remaps Int 10H Function 01H cursor starting and ending lines for the
current character cell dimensions.

Call with:

AH	= 12H
AL	= 00H to enable cursor emulation
	01H to disable cursor emulation
BL	= 34H

Returns:

If function supported
AL   = 12H

Int 10H Function 12H [MCGA] [VGA]
Subfunction 35H
Switch Active Display

Allows selection of one of two video adapters in the system, when
memory usage or port addresses conflict between the two adapters.

Call with:

AH	= 12H
AL	= switching function
	00H to disable initial video adapter
	01H to enable system board video adapter
	02H to disable active video adapter
	03H to enable inactive video adapter
BL	= 35H
ES:DX	= segment:offset of 128-byte buffer (if AL = 00H, 02H, or 03H)

Returns:

If function supported
AL   = 12H

and, if called with AL = 00H or 02H
Video adapter state information saved in caller's buffer

or, if called with AL = 03H
Video adapter state restored from information in caller's buffer.

Notes:

- This subfunction cannot be used unless both video adapters have a disable capability (Int 10H Function 12H Subfunction 32H).

- If there is no conflict between the system board video and the adapter board video in memory or port usage, both video controllers can be active simultaneously and this subfunction is not required.

Int 10H Function 12H   [VGA]
Subfunction 36H
Enable/Disable Screen Refresh

Enables or disables the video refresh for the currently active display.

Call with:

AH   = 12H
AL   = 00H to enable refresh
         01H to disable refresh
BL   = 36H

Returns:

If function supported
AL   = 12H

Int 10H Function 13H
Write String in
Teletype Mode

[MDA] [CGA] [PCjr]
[EGA] [MCGA] [VGA]

Transfers a string to the video buffer for the currently active display, starting at the specified position.

Call with:

AH	= 13H
AL	= write mode

	0	*attribute in BL;*
		string contains character codes only; and
		cursor position is not updated after write
	1	*attribute in BL;*
		string contains character codes only; and
		cursor position is updated after write
	2	*string contains alternating character codes*
		and attribute bytes; and
		cursor position is not updated after write
	3	*string contains alternating character codes*
		and attribute bytes; and
		cursor position is updated after write

BH	= page
BL	= attribute, if AL = 00H or 01H
CX	= length of character string
DH	= *y* coordinate (row)
DL	= *x* coordinate (column)
ES:BP	= segment:offset of string

Returns:

Nothing

Notes:

■ This function is not available on the original IBM PC or PC/XT unless an EGA video adapter (which contains its own ROM BIOS) is installed.

■ This function can be thought of as an extension to Int 10H Function 0EH. The control characters bell (07H), backspace (08H), line feed (0AH), and carriage return (0DH) are recognized and handled appropriately.

Int 10H Function 1AH
[PS/2]
Get or Set Display Combination Code

Returns a code describing the installed display adapter(s), or updates the ROM BIOS's variable describing the installed adapter(s).

Call with:

AH	= 1AH
AL	= subfunction
	00H = get display combination code
	01H = set display combination code
BH	= inactive display code (if AL = 01H)
BL	= active display code (if AL = 01H)

Returns:

If function supported
AL   = 1AH

and, if called with AL = 00H
BH   = inactive display code
BL   = active display code

Note:

■ The display codes are interpreted as follows:

Code(s)	Video Subsystem Type
00H	no display
01H	MDA with 5151 monitor
02H	CGA with 5153 or 5154 monitor
03H	reserved
04H	EGA with 5153 or 5154 monitor
05H	EGA with 5151 monitor
06H	PGA with 5175 monitor
07H	VGA with analog monochrome monitor
08H	VGA with analog color monitor
09H	reserved
0AH	MCGA with digital color monitor
0BH	MCGA with analog monochrome monitor

(continued)

Code(s)	Video Subsystem Type
0CH	MCGA with analog color monitor
0DH–FEH	reserved
FFH	unknown

Int 10H Function 1BH [PS/2]
Get Functionality/State Information

Obtains information about the current display mode, as well as a pointer to a table describing the characteristics and capabilities of the video adapter and monitor.

Call with:

AH	= 1BH
BX	= implementation type (always 00H)
ES:DI	= segment:offset of 64-byte buffer

Returns:

If function supported
AL   = 1BH

and information placed in caller's buffer (see Notes)

Notes:

- The caller's buffer is filled in with information that depends on the current video display mode:

Byte(s)	Contents
00H–03H	pointer to functionality information (see next Note)
04H	current video mode
05H–06H	number of character columns
07H–08H	length of video refresh buffer (bytes)
09H–0AH	starting address in buffer of upper left corner of display
0BH–1AH	cursor position for video pages 0–7 as eight 2-byte entries; first byte of each pair is y coordinate, second byte is x coordinate
1BH	cursor starting line
1CH	cursor ending line

(continued)

Byte(s)	Contents
1DH	active display page
1EH–1FH	adapter base port address (3BXH monochrome, 3DXH color)
20H	current setting of register 3B8H or 3D8H
21H	current setting of register 3B9H or 3D9H
22H	number of character rows
23H–24H	character height in scan lines
25H	active display code (see Int 10H Function 1AH)
26H	inactive display code (see Int 10H Function 1AH)
27H–28H	number of displayable colors (0 for monochrome)
29H	number of display pages
2AH	number of scan lines

00H	*= 200 scan lines*
01H	*= 350 scan lines*
02H	*= 400 scan lines*
03H	*= 480 scan lines*
04H–FFH	*= reserved*

Byte(s)	Contents
2BH	primary character block (see Int 10H Function 11H Subfunction 03H)
2CH	secondary character block
2DH	miscellaneous state information

Bit(s)	*Significance*
0	*= 1 if all modes on all displays active (always 0 on MCGA)*
1	*= 1 if gray-scale summing active*
2	*= 1 if monochrome display attached*
3	*= 1 if mode set default palette loading disabled*
4	*= 1 if cursor emulation active (always 0 on MCGA)*
5	*= state of I/B toggle (0=intensity, 1=blink)*
6–7	*= reserved*

Byte(s)	Contents
2EH–30H	reserved

(continued)

Byte(s)	Contents		
31H	video memory available		
	00H	= 64 KB	
	01H	= 128 KB	
	02H	= 192 KB	
	03H	= 256 KB	
32H	save pointer state information		
	Bit(s)	Significance	
	0	= 1 if 512-character set active	
	1	= 1 if dynamic save area active	
	2	= 1 if alpha font override active	
	3	= 1 if graphics font override active	
	4	= 1 if palette override active	
	5	= 1 if display combination code (DCC) extension active	
	6–7	= reserved	
33H–3FH	reserved		

■ Bytes 0–3 of the caller's buffer contain a DWORD pointer (offset in lower word, segment in upper word) to the following information about the display adapter and monitor:

Byte(s)	Contents	
00H	video modes supported	
	Bit	Significance
	0	= 1 if mode 00H supported
	1	= 1 if mode 01H supported
	2	= 1 if mode 02H supported
	3	= 1 if mode 03H supported
	4	= 1 if mode 04H supported
	5	= 1 if mode 05H supported
	6	= 1 if mode 06H supported
	7	= 1 if mode 07H supported
01H	video modes supported	
	Bit	Significance
	0	= 1 if mode 08H supported
	1	= 1 if mode 09H supported
	2	= 1 if mode 0AH supported

(continued)

Byte(s)	Contents
	3 = 1 if mode 0BH supported
	4 = 1 if mode 0CH supported
	5 = 1 if mode 0DH supported
	6 = 1 if mode 0EH supported
	7 = 1 if mode 0FH supported
02H	video modes supported

Bit(s) *Significance*

0 = 1 if mode 10H supported

1 = 1 if mode 11H supported

2 = 1 if mode 12H supported

3 = 1 if mode 13H supported

4–7 = reserved

03H–06H	reserved
07H	scan lines available in text modes

Bit(s) *Significance*

0 = 1 if 200 scan lines

1 = 1 if 350 scan lines

2 = 1 if 400 scan lines

3–7 = reserved

08H	character blocks available in text modes (see Int 10H Function 11H)
09H	maximum number of active character blocks in text modes
0AH	miscellaneous BIOS capabilities

Bit *Significance*

0 = 1 if all modes active on all displays (always 0 for MCGA)

1 = 1 if gray-scale summing available

2 = 1 if character font loading available

3 = 1 if mode set default palette loading available

4 = 1 if cursor emulation available

5 = 1 if EGA (64-color) palette available

6 = 1 if color register loading available

7 = 1 if color register paging mode select available

(continued)

Byte(s)	Contents
0BH	miscellaneous BIOS capabilities

Bit(s)	Significance
0	= 1 if light pen available
1	= 1 if save/restore video state available (always 0 on MCGA)
2	= 1 if background intensity/blinking control available
3	= 1 if get/set display combination code available
4–7	= reserved

Byte(s)	Contents
0CH–0DH	reserved
0EH	save area capabilities

Bit(s)	Significance
0	= 1 if supports 512-character sets
1	= 1 if dynamic save area available
2	= 1 if alpha font override available
3	= 1 if graphics font override available
4	= 1 if palette override available
5	= 1 if display combination code extension available
6–7	= reserved

Byte(s)	Contents
0FH	reserved

Int 10H Function 1CH [PS/2]
Save or Restore Video State

Saves or restores the digital-to-analog converter (DAC) state and color
registers, ROM BIOS video driver data area, or video hardware state.

Call with:

AH	= 1CH
AL	= subfunction
	00H to get state buffer size
	01H to save state
	02H to restore state
CX	= requested states

Bit(s)	Significance (if set)
0	*save/restore video hardware state*
1	*save/restore video BIOS data area*
2	*save/restore video DAC state and color registers*
3–15	*reserved*

ES:BX = segment:offset of buffer

Returns:

If function supported
AL = 1CH

and, if called with AL = 00H
BX = buffer block count (64 bytes per block)

or, if called with AL = 01H
State information placed in caller's buffer

or, if called with AL = 02H
Requested state restored according to contents of caller's buffer

Notes:

■ Subfunction 00H is used to determine the size of buffer that will be necessary to contain the specified state information. The caller must supply the buffer.

■ The current video state is altered during a save state operation (AL = 01H). If the requesting program needs to continue in the same video state, it can follow the save state request with an immediate call to restore the video state.

■ This function is supported on the VGA only.

Int 11H   [PC] [AT] [PS/2]
Get Equipment Configuration

Obtains the equipment list code word from the ROM BIOS.

Call with:

Nothing

Returns:

AX = equipment list code word

Bit(s)	Significance
14–15	*number of printers installed*

(continued)

Bit(s)	Significance
13	= 1 if internal modem installed (PC and XT only)
	= 1 if serial printer attached (PCjr)
12	= 1 if game adapter installed
9–11	number of RS-232 ports installed
8	reserved
6–7	number of floppy disk drives (if bit 0 = 1)
	00 = 1
	01 = 2
	10 = 3
	11 = 4
4–5	initial video mode
	00 reserved
	01 40-by-25 color text
	10 80-by-25 color text
	11 80-by-25 monochrome
2–3	system board RAM size (PC, see Note)
	00 = 16 KB
	01 = 32 KB
	10 = 48 KB
	11 = 64 KB
2	= 1 if pointing device installed (PS/2)
1	= 1 if math coprocessor installed
0	= 1 if floppy disk drive(s) installed

Note:

- Bits 2–3 of the returned value are used only in the ROM BIOS for the original IBM PC with the 64 KB system board and on the PCjr.

Int 12H [PC] [AT] [PS/2]
Get Conventional Memory Size

Returns the amount of conventional memory available for use by MS-DOS and application programs.

Call with:

Nothing

Returns:

AX   = memory size (in KB)

- On some early PC models, the amount of memory returned by this function is controlled by the settings of the dip switches on the system board and may not reflect all the memory that is physically present.

- On the PC/AT, the value returned is the amount of *functional* memory found during the power-on self-test, regardless of the memory size configuration information stored in CMOS RAM.

- The value returned does not reflect any extended memory (above the 1 MB boundary) that may be installed on 80286 or 80386 machines such as the PC/AT or PS/2 (Models 50 and above).

Int 13H Function 00H [PC] [AT] [PS/2]
Reset Disk System

Resets the disk controller, recalibrates its attached drives (the read/write arm is moved to cylinder 0), and prepares for disk I/O.

Call with:

AH	= 00H
DL	= drive
	00H–7FH *floppy disk*
	80H–FFH *fixed disk*

Returns:

If function successful
Carry flag = clear
AH   = 00H

If function unsuccessful
Carry flag = set
AH   = status (see Int 13H Function 01H)

Notes:

- This function should be called after a failed floppy disk Read, Write, Verify, or Format request before retrying the operation.

- If called with DL > = 80H (i.e., selecting a fixed disk drive), the floppy disk controller and then the fixed disk controller are reset. See also Int 13H Function 0DH, which allows the fixed disk controller to be reset without affecting the floppy disk controller.

Int 13H Function 01H   [PC] [AT] [PS/2]
Get Disk System Status

Returns the status of the most recent disk operation.

Call with:

AH	= 01H
DL	= drive

          00H–7FH   *floppy disk*
          80H–FFH   *fixed disk*

Returns:

AH	= 00H
AL	= status of previous disk operation

00H	*no error*
01H	*invalid command*
02H	*address mark not found*
03H	*disk write-protected (F)*
04H	*sector not found*
05H	*reset failed (H)*
06H	*floppy disk removed (F)*
07H	*bad parameter table (H)*
08H	*DMA overrun (F)*
09H	*DMA crossed 64 KB boundary*
0AH	*bad sector flag (H)*
0BH	*bad track flag (H)*
0CH	*media type not found (F)*
0DH	*invalid number of sectors on format (H)*
0EH	*control data address mark detected (H)*
0FH	*DMA arbitration level out of range (H)*
10H	*uncorrectable CRC[1] or ECC[2] data error*
11H	*ECC corrected data error (H)*
20H	*controller failed*
40H	*seek failed*
80H	*disk timedout (failed to respond)*
AAH	*drive not ready (H)*
BBH	*undefined error (H)*
CCH	*write fault (H)*
E0H	*status register error (H)*
FFH	*sense operation failed (H)*

H=fixed disk only, F=floppy disk only

[1] Cyclic Redundancy Check code
[2] Error Checking and Correcting code

Note:

■ On fixed disks, error code 11H (ECC data error) indicates that a recoverable error was detected during a preceding Read Sector (Int 13H Function 02H) function.

Int 13H Function 02H [PC] [AT] [PS/2]
Read Sector

Reads one or more sectors from disk into memory.

Call with:

AH	= 02H
AL	= number of sectors
CH	= cylinder
CL	= sector
DH	= head
DL	= drive
	00H–7FH floppy disk
	80H–FFH fixed disk
ES:BX	= segment:offset of buffer

Returns:

If function successful
Carry flag   = clear
AH   = 00H
AL   = number of sectors transferred

If function unsuccessful
Carry flag   = set
AH   = status (see Int 13H Function 01H)

Notes:

■ On fixed disks, the upper 2 bits of the 10-bit cylinder number are placed in the upper 2 bits of register CL.

■ On fixed disks, error code 11H indicates that a read error occurred that was corrected by the ECC algorithm; in this event, register AL contains the burst length. The data returned is probably good, although there is a small chance that the data was not corrected properly. If a multisector transfer was requested, the operation was terminated after the sector containing the read error.

■ On floppy disk drives, an error may result from the drive motor being off at the time of the request. The ROM BIOS does not automatically wait for the drive to come up to speed before attempting the read operation. The requesting program should reset the floppy disk system (Int 13H Function 00H) and retry the operation three times before assuming that the error results from some other cause.

Int 13H Function 03H   [PC] [AT] [PS/2]
Write Sector

Writes one or more sectors from memory to disk.

Call with:

AH	= 03H
AL	= number of sectors
CH	= cylinder
CL	= sector
DH	= head
DL	= drive
	00H−7FH floppy disk
	80H−FFH fixed disk
ES:BX	= segment:offset of buffer

Returns:

If function successful
Carry flag = clear
AH = 00H
AL = number of sectors transferred

If function unsuccessful
Carry flag = set
AH = status (see Int 13H Function 01H)

Notes:

■ On fixed disks, the upper 2 bits of the 10-bit cylinder number are placed in the upper 2 bits of register CL.

■ On floppy disk drives, an error may result from the drive motor being off at the time of the request. The ROM BIOS does not automatically wait for the drive to come up to speed before attempting the write operation. The requesting program should reset the floppy disk system (Int 13H Function 00H) and retry the operation three times before assuming that the error results from some other cause.

Int 13H Function 04H [PC] [AT] [PS/2]
Verify Sector

Verifies the address fields of one or more sectors. No data is transferred to or from memory by this operation.

Call with:

AH	= 04H
AL	= number of sectors
CH	= cylinder
CL	= sector
DH	= head
DL	= drive
	00H–7FH floppy disk
	80H–FFH fixed disk
ES:BX	= segment:offset of buffer (see Notes)

Returns:

If function successful
Carry flag = clear
AH   = 00H
AL   = number of sectors verified

If function unsuccessful
Carry flag = set
AH   = status (see Int 13H Function 01H)

Notes:

- On PCs, PC/XTs, and PC/ATs with ROM BIOS dated earlier than 11/15/85, ES:BX should point to a valid buffer.

- On fixed disks, the upper 2 bits of the 10-bit cylinder number are placed in the upper 2 bits of register CL.

- This function can be used to test whether a readable media is in a floppy disk drive. An error may result from the drive motor being off at the time of the request, because the ROM BIOS does not automatically wait for the drive to come up to speed before attempting the verify operation. The requesting program should reset the floppy disk system (Int 13H Function 00H) and retry the operation three times before assuming that a readable floppy disk is not present.

Int 13H Function 05H　　　　[PC] [AT] [PS/2]
Format Track

Initializes disk sector and track address fields on the specified track.

Call with:

AH	= 05H
AL	= interleave (PC/XT fixed disks)
CH	= cylinder
DH	= head
DL	= drive
	00H–7FH　floppy disk
	80H–FFH　fixed disk
ES:BX	= segment:offset of address field list (except PC/XT fixed disk, see Notes)

Returns:

If function successful
Carry flag　= clear
AH　　　　 = 00H

If function unsuccessful
Carry flag　= set
AH　　　　 = status (see Int 13H Function 01H)

Notes:

■ On floppy disks, the address field list consists of a series of 4-byte entries, one entry per sector, in the following format:

Byte	Contents
0	cylinder
1	head
2	sector
3	sector-size code
	00H　　if 128 bytes per sector
	01H　　if 256 bytes per sector
	02H　　if 512 bytes per sector (standard)
	03H　　if 1024 bytes per sector

■ On floppy disks, the number of sectors per track is taken from the BIOS floppy disk parameter table whose address is stored in the vector for Int 1EH.

- When this function is used for floppy disks on the PC/AT or PS/2, it should be preceded by a call to Int 13H Function 17H to select the type of medium to be formatted.

- On fixed disks, the upper 2 bits of the 10-bit cylinder number are placed in the upper 2 bits of register CL.

- On PC/XT-286, PC/AT, and PS/2 fixed disks, ES:BX points to a 512-byte buffer containing byte pairs for each physical disk sector as follows:

Byte	Contents
0	00H for good sector
	80H for bad sector
1	sector number

For example, to format a track with 17 sectors and an interleave of two, ES:BX would point to the following 34-byte array at the beginning of a 512-byte buffer:

```
db    00h,01h,00h,0ah,00h,02h,00h,0bh,00h,03h,00h,0ch
db    00h,04h,00h,0dh,00h,05h,00h,0eh,00h,06h,00h,0fh
db    00h,07h,00h,10h,00h,08h,00h,11h,00h,09h
```

Int 13H Function 06H [PC]
Format Bad Track

Initializes a track, writing disk address fields and data sectors and setting bad sector flags.

Call with:

AH	= 06H
AL	= interleave
CH	= cylinder
DH	= head
DL	= drive
	80H–FFH fixed disk

Returns:

If function successful
Carry flag = clear
AH   = 00H

If function unsuccessful
Carry flag = set
AH   = status (see Int 13H Function 01H)

Notes:

■ This function is defined for PC/XT fixed disk drives only.

■ For additional information, see Notes for Int 13H Function 05H.

Int 13H Function 07H [PC]
Format Drive

Formats the entire drive, writing disk address fields and data sectors, starting at the specified cylinder.

Call with:

AH	= 07H
AL	= interleave
CH	= cylinder
DL	= drive
	80H–FFH fixed disk

Returns:

If function successful
Carry flag = clear
AH   = 00H

If function unsuccessful
Carry flag = set
AH   = status (see Int 13H Function 01H)

Notes:

■ This function is defined for PC/XT fixed disk drives only.

■ For additional information, see Notes for Int 13H Function 05H.

Int 13H Function 08H [PC] [AT] [PS/2]
Get Drive Parameters

Returns various parameters for the specified drive.

Call with:

AH	= 08H
DL	= drive
	00H–7FH floppy disk
	80H–FFH fixed disk

Returns:

If function successful
Carry flag = clear
BL   = drive type (PC/AT and PS/2 floppy disks)
    01H if 360 KB, 40 track, 5.25"
    02H if 1.2 MB, 80 track, 5.25"
    03H if 720 KB, 80 track, 3.5"
    04H if 1.44 MB, 80 track, 3.5"
CH   = low 8 bits of maximum cylinder number
CL   = bits 6–7 high-order 2 bits of maximum cylinder
         number
    bits 0–5 maximum sector number
DH   = maximum head number
DL   = number of drives
ES:DI   = segment:offset of disk drive parameter table

If function unsuccessful
Carry flag = set
AH   = status (see Int 13H Function 01H)

Notes:

- On the PC and PC/XT, this function is supported on fixed disks only.

- The value returned in register DL reflects the true number of physical drives attached to the adapter for the requested drive.

Int 13H Function 09H   [PC] [AT] [PS/2]
Initialize Fixed Disk
Characteristics

Initializes the fixed disk controller for subsequent I/O operations, using the values found in the ROM BIOS disk parameter block(s).

Call with:

AH = 09H
DL = drive
    80H–FFH fixed disk

and, on the PC/XT
Vector for Int 41H must point to disk parameter block

or, on the PC/AT and PS/2
Vector for Int 41H must point to disk parameter block for drive 0
Vector for Int 46H must point to disk parameter block for drive 1

Returns:

If function successful
Carry flag = clear
AH   = 00H

If function unsuccessful
Carry flag = set
AH   = status (see Int 13H Function 01H)

Notes:

- This function is supported on fixed disks only.
- For PC and PC/XT fixed disks, the parameter block format is as follows:

Byte(s)	*Contents*
00H–01H	maximum number of cylinders
02H	maximum number of heads
03H–04H	starting reduced write current cylinder
05H–06H	starting write precompensation cylinder
07H	maximum ECC burst length
08H	drive options
	bit 7 = 1 if disable disk-access retries
	bit 6 = 1 if disable ECC retries
	bits 3–5 = 0
	bits 0–2 = drive option
09H	standard time-out value
0AH	time-out value for format drive
0BH	time-out value for check drive
0CH–0FH	reserved

- For PC/AT and PS/2 fixed disks, the parameter block format is as follows:

Byte(s)	*Contents*
00H–01H	maximum number of cylinders
02H	maximum number of heads
03H–04H	reserved
05H–06H	starting write precompensation cylinder
07H	maximum ECC burst length

(continued)

Byte(s)	Contents
08H	drive options
	bits 6–7 = nonzero (10, 01, or 11) if retries disabled
	bit 5 = 1 if manufacturer's defect map present at maximum cylinder + 1
	bit 4 = not used
	bit 3 = 1 if more than 8 heads
	bits 0–2 = not used
09H–0BH	reserved
0CH–0DH	landing zone cylinder
0EH	sectors per track
0FH	reserved

Int 13H Function 0AH [PC] [AT] [PS/2]
Read Sector Long

Reads a sector or sectors from disk into memory, along with a 4-byte ECC code for each sector.

Call with:

AH	= 0AH
AL	= number of sectors
CH	= cylinder
CL	= sector (see Notes)
DH	= head
DL	= drive
	80H–FFH fixed disk
ES:BX	= segment:offset of buffer

Returns:

If function successful

Carry flag	= clear
AH	= 00H
AL	= number of sectors transferred

If function unsuccessful

Carry flag	= set
AH	= status (see Int 13H Function 01H)

Notes:

- This function is supported on fixed disks only.

- The upper 2 bits of the 10-bit cylinder number are placed in the upper 2 bits of register CL.

- Unlike the normal Read Sector function (Int 13H Function 02H), ECC errors are not automatically corrected. Multisector transfers are terminated after any sector with a read error.

Int 13H Function 0BH   [PC] [AT] [PS/2]
Write Sector Long

Writes a sector or sectors from memory to disk. Each sector's worth of data must be followed by its 4-byte ECC code.

Call with:

AH	= 0BH
AL	= number of sectors
CH	= cylinder
CL	= sector (see Notes)
DH	= head
DL	= drive
	80H–FFH fixed disk
ES:BX	= segment:offset of buffer

Returns:

If function successful
Carry flag = clear
AH   = 00H
AL   = number of sectors transferred

If function unsuccessful
Carry flag = set
AH   = status (see Int 13H Function 01H)

Notes:

- This function is supported on fixed disks only.

- The upper 2 bits of the 10-bit cylinder number are placed in the upper 2 bits of register CL.

Int 13H Function 0CH
Seek

Positions the disk read/write heads to the specified cylinder, but does not transfer any data.

Call with:

AH	= 0CH
CH	= lower 8 bits of cylinder
CL	= upper 2 bits of cylinder in bits 6–7
DH	= head
DL	= drive
	80H–FFH fixed disk

Returns:

If function successful
Carry flag = clear
AH   = 00H

If function unsuccessful
Carry flag = set
AH   = status (see Int 13H Function 01H)

Notes:

■ This function is supported on fixed disks only.

■ The upper 2 bits of the 10-bit cylinder number are placed in the upper 2 bits of register CL.

■ The Read Sector, Read Sector Long, Write Sector, and Write Sector Long functions include an implied seek operation and need not be preceded by an explicit call to this function.

Int 13H Function 0DH
Reset Fixed Disk System

[PC] [AT] [PS/2]

Resets the fixed disk controller, recalibrates attached drives (moves the read/write arm to cylinder 0), and prepares for subsequent disk I/O.

Call with:

AH	= 0DH
DL	= drive
	80H–FFH *fixed disk*

Returns:

If function successful
Carry flag = clear
AH = 00H

If function unsuccessful
Carry flag = set
AH = status (see Int 13H Function 01H)

Note:

■ This function is supported on fixed disks only. It differs from Int 13H Function 00H in that the floppy disk controller is not reset.

Int 13H Function 0EH [PC]
Read Sector Buffer

Transfers the contents of the fixed disk adapter's internal sector buffer to system memory. No data is read from the physical disk drive.

Call with:

AH	= 0EH
ES:BX	= segment:offset of buffer

Returns:

If function successful
Carry flag = clear

If function unsuccessful
Carry flag = set
AH = status (see Int 13H Function 01H)

Note:

■ This function is supported by the PC/XT's fixed disk adapter only. It is not defined for fixed disk adapters on the PC/AT or PS/2.

Int 13H Function 0FH [PC]
Write Sector Buffer

Transfers data from system memory to the fixed disk adapter's internal sector buffer. No data is written to the physical disk drive.

Call with:

AH	= 0FH
ES:BX	= segment:offset of buffer

Returns:

If function successful
Carry flag = clear

If function unsuccessful
Carry flag = set
AH = status (see Int 13H Function 01H)

Notes:

■ This function is supported by the PC/XT's fixed disk adapter only. It is not defined for fixed disk adapters on the PC/AT or PS/2.

■ This function should be called to initialize the contents of the sector buffer before formatting the drive with Int 13H Function 05H.

Int 13H Function 10H [PC] [AT] [PS/2]
Get Drive Status

Tests whether the specified fixed disk drive is operational and returns the drive's status.

Call with:

AH	= 10H
DL	= drive
	80H–FFH fixed disk

Returns:

If function successful
Carry flag = clear
AH = 00H

If function unsuccessful
Carry flag = set
AH = status (see Int 13H Function 01H)

Note:

- This function is supported on fixed disks only.

Int 13H Function 11H [PC] [AT] [PS/2]
Recalibrate Drive

Causes the fixed disk adapter to recalibrate itself for the specified drive, positioning the read/arm to cylinder 0, and returns the drive's status.

Call with:

AH = 11H
DL = drive
  80H–FFH   fixed disk

Returns:

If function successful
Carry flag = clear
AH = 00H

If function unsuccessful
Carry flag = set
AH = status (see Int 13H Function 01H)

Note:

- This function is supported on fixed disks only.

Int 13H Function 12H [PC]
Controller RAM Diagnostic

Causes the fixed disk adapter to carry out a built-in diagnostic test on its internal sector buffer, indicating whether the test was passed by the returned status.

Call with:

AH = 12H

Returns:

If function successful
Carry flag = clear

If function unsuccessful
Carry flag = set
AH   = status (see Int 13H Function 01H)

Note:

■ This function is supported on PC/XT fixed disks only.

Int 13H Function 13H [PC]
Controller Drive Diagnostic

Causes the fixed disk adapter to run internal diagnostic tests of the attached drive, indicating whether the test was passed by the returned status.

Call with:

AH   = 13H

Returns:

If function successful
Carry flag = clear

If function unsuccessful
Carry flag = set
AH   = status (see Int 13H Function 01H)

Note:

■ This function is supported on PC/XT fixed disks only.

Int 13H Function 14H [PC] [AT] [PS/2]
Controller Internal Diagnostic

Causes the fixed disk adapter to carry out a built-in diagnostic self-test, indicating whether the test was passed by the returned status.

Call with:

AH = 14H

Returns:

If function successful
Carry flag = clear
AH = 00H

If function unsuccessful
Carry flag = set
AH = status (see Int 13H Function 01H)

Note:

■ This function is supported on fixed disks only.

Int 13H Function 15H [AT] [PS/2]
Get Disk Type

Returns a code indicating the type of floppy or fixed disk referenced by the specified drive code.

Call with:

AH = 15H
DL = drive

    00H–7FH   floppy disk
    80H–FFH   fixed disk

Returns:

If function successful
Carry flag = clear
AH = drive type code

    00H   if no drive present
    01H   if floppy disk drive without change-line support
    02H   if floppy disk drive with change-line support
    03H   if fixed disk

and, if fixed disk (AH = 03H)
CX:DX = number of 512-byte sectors

If function unsuccessful
Carry flag = set
AH = status (see Int 13H Function 01H)

Note:

■ This function is not supported on the PC or PC/XT.

Int 13H Function 16H   [AT] [PS/2]
Get Disk Change Status

Returns the status of the change line, indicating whether the disk in the drive may have been replaced since the last disk access.

Call with:

AH	= 16H
DL	= drive
	00H–7FH *floppy disk*

Returns:

If change line inactive (disk has not been changed)
Carry flag = clear
AH   = 00H

If change line active (disk may have been changed)
Carry flag = set
AH   = 06H

Notes:

■ If this function returns with the carry flag set, the disk has not necessarily been changed; the change line can be activated by simply unlocking and locking the disk drive door without removing the floppy disk.

■ This function is not supported for floppy disks on the PC or PC/XT.

Int 13H Function 17H   [AT] [PS/2]
Set Disk Type

Selects a floppy disk type for the specified drive.

Call with:

AH	= 17H
AL	= floppy disk type code

> 00H   *not used*
> 01H   *320/360 KB floppy disk in 360 KB drive*
> 02H   *320/360 KB floppy disk in 1.2 MB drive*
> 03H   *1.2 MB floppy disk in 1.2 MB drive*
> 04H   *720 KB floppy disk in 720 KB drive*

DL	= drive

> 00H–7FH   *floppy disk*

Returns:

If function successful

Carry flag	= clear
AH	= 00H

If function unsuccessful

Carry flag	= set
AH	= status (see Int 13H Function 01H)

Notes:

- This function is not supported for floppy disks on the PC or PC/XT.

- If the change line is active for the specified drive, it is reset. The ROM BIOS then sets the data rate for the specified drive and media type.

Int 13H Function 18H   [AT] [PS/2]
Set Media Type for Format

Selects media characteristics for the specified drive.

Call with:

AH	= 18H
CH	= number of cylinders
CL	= sectors per track
DL	= drive

> 00H–7FH   *floppy disk*

Returns:

If function successful
Carry flag = clear
AH   = 00H
ES:DI   = segment:offset of disk parameter table for media type

If function unsuccessful
Carry flag = set
AH   = status (see Int 13H Function 01H)

Notes:

- A floppy disk must be present in the drive.

- This function should be called prior to formatting a disk with Int 13H Function 05H so that the ROM BIOS can set the correct data rate for the media.

- If the change line is active for the specified drive, it is reset.

Int 13H Function 19H [PS/2]
Park Heads

Moves the read/write arm to a track that is not used for data storage, so that data will not be damaged when the drive is turned off.

Call with:

AH   = 19H
DL   = drive
              80H–FFH   fixed disk

Returns:

If function successful
Carry flag = clear
AH   = 00H

If function unsuccessful
Carry flag = set
AH   = status (see Int 13H Function 01H)

Note:

- This function is defined for PS/2 fixed disks only.

Int 13H Function 1AH
Format ESDI Drive

Initializes disk sector and track address fields on a drive attached to
the ESDI Fixed Disk Drive Adapter/A.

Call with:

AH	= 1AH
AL	= relative block address (RBA) defect table count
	0 if no RBA table
	>0 if RBA table used
CL	= format modifier bits
	Bit(s) Significance (if set)
	0 ignore primary defect map
	1 ignore secondary defect map
	2 update secondary defect map (see Notes)
	3 perform extended surface analysis
	4 generate periodic interrupt (see Notes)
	5–7 reserved (must be 0)
DL	= drive
	80H–FFH fixed disk
ES:BX	= segment:offset of RBA table

Returns:

If function successful
Carry flag   = clear
AH   = 00H

If function unsuccessful
Carry flag   = set
AH   = status (see Int 13H Function 01H)

Notes:

- This operation is sometimes called a "low level format" and prepares the disk for physical read/write operations at the sector level.
The drive must be subsequently partitioned with the FDISK command and then given a "high level format" with the FORMAT
command to install a file system.

- If bit 4 of register CL is set, Int 15H is called with AH = 0FH and
AL = phase code after each cylinder is formatted or analyzed. The
phase code is defined as:

0 = reserved
1 = surface analysis

(continued)

2 = formatting

See also Int 15H Function 0FH.

■ If bit 2 of register CL is set, the drive's secondary defect map is updated to reflect errors found during surface analysis. If both bit 2 and bit 1 are set, the secondary defect map is replaced.

■ For an extended surface analysis, the disk should first be formatted by calling this function with bit 3 cleared and then analyzed by calling this function with bit 3 set.

Int 14H Function 00H   [PC] [AT] [PS/2]
Initialize Communications Port

Initializes a serial communications port to a desired baud rate, parity, word length, and number of stop bits.

Call with:

AH	= 00H
AL	= initialization parameter (see Notes)
DX	= communications port number (0 = COM1, 1 = COM2, etc.)

Returns:

AH = port status

Bit	Significance (if set)
7	timed-out
6	transmit shift register empty
5	transmit holding register empty
4	break detected
3	framing error detected
2	parity error detected
1	overrun error detected
0	receive data ready

AL = modem status

Bit	Significance (if set)
7	receive line signal detect
6	ring indicator
5	data-set-ready
4	clear-to-send
3	change in receive line signal detect
2	trailing edge ring indicator
1	change in data-set-ready status
0	change in clear-to-send status

Notes:

- The initialization parameter byte is defined as follows:

7 6 5 *Baud Rate*	4 3 *Parity*	2 *Stop Bits*	1 0 *Word Length*
000 = 110	X0 = none	0 = 1 bit	10 = 7 bits
001 = 150	01 = odd	1 = 2 bits	11 = 8 bits
010 = 300	11 = even		
011 = 600			
100 = 1200			
101 = 2400			
110 = 4800			
111 = 9600			

- To initialize the serial port for data rates greater than 9600 baud on PS/2 machines, see Int 14H Functions 04H and 05H.

Int 14H Function 01H   [PC] [AT] [PS/2]
Write Character to Communications Port

Writes a character to the specified serial communications port, returning the current status of the port.

Call with:

AH	= 01H
AL	= character
DX	= communications port number (0 = COM1, 1 = COM2, etc.)

Returns:

If function successful

AH bit 7 = 0
AH bits 0–6 = port status

Bit	Significance (if set)
6	transmit shift register empty
5	transmit holding register empty
4	break detected
3	framing error detected
2	parity error detected
1	overrun error detected
0	receive data ready

| AL | = character (unchanged) |

If function unsuccessful (timed-out)

| AH bit 7 | = 1 |
| AL | = character (unchanged) |

Int 14H Function 02H [PC] [AT] [PS/2]
Read Character from
Communications Port

Reads a character from the specified serial communications port, also returning the port's status.

Call with:

AH	= 02H
DX	= communications port number (0 = COM1,
	1 = COM2, etc.)

Returns:

If function successful

| AH bit 7 | = 0 |
| AH bits 0–6 | = status |

Bit	Significance (if set)
4	break detected
3	framing error detected
2	parity error detected
1	overrun error detected

| AL | = character |

If function unsuccessful (timed-out)

| AH bit 7 | = 1 |

Int 14H Function 03H [PC] [AT] [PS/2]
Get Communications Port Status

Returns the status of the specified serial communications port.

Call with:

AH	= 03H
DX	= communications port number (0 = COM1,
	1 = COM2, etc.)

Returns:

AH   = port status (see Int 14H Function 00H)
AL   = modem status (see Int 14H Function 00H)

Int 14H Function 04H   [PS/2]
Extended Initialize Communications Port

Initializes a serial communications port to a desired baud rate, parity, word length, and number of stop bits. Provides a superset of Int 14H Function 00H capabilities for PS/2 machines.

Call with:

AH	= 04H
AL	= break flag
	00H *no break*
	01H *break*
BH	= parity
	00H *none*
	01H *odd*
	02H *even*
	03H *stick parity odd*
	04H *stick parity even*
BL	= stop bits
	00H *1 stop bit*
	01H *2 stop bits if word length = 6–8 bits*
	01H *1.5 stop bits if word length = 5 bits*
CH	= word length
	00H *5 bits*
	01H *6 bits*
	02H *7 bits*
	03H *8 bits*
CL	= baud rate
	00H *110 baud*
	01H *150 baud*
	02H *300 baud*
	03H *600 baud*
	04H *1200 baud*
	05H *2400 baud*
	06H *4800 baud*
	07H *9600 baud*
	08H *19,200 baud*
DX	= communications port number (0 = COM1, 1 = COM2, etc.)

AH	= port status (see Int 14H Function 00H)
AL	= modem status (see Int 14H Function 00H)

Int 14H Function 05H [PS/2]
Extended Communications Port Control

Reads or sets the modem control register (MCR) for the specified serial communications port.

Call with:

AH	= 05H
AL	= subfunction
	00H to read modem control register
	01H to write modem control register
BL	= modem control register contents (if AL = 01H)
	Bit(s) Significance
	0 data-terminal ready
	1 request-to-send
	2 Out1
	3 Out2
	4 loop (for testing)
	5–7 reserved
DX	= communications port number (0 = COM1, 1 = COM2, etc.)

Returns:

If called with AL = 00H

BL	= modem control register contents (see above)

If called with AL = 01H

AH	= port status (see Int 14H Function 00H)
AL	= modem status (see Int 14H Function 00H)

Int 15H Function 00H [PC]
Turn On Cassette Motor

Turns on the motor of the cassette tape drive.

Call with:

AH	= 00H

Returns:

If function successful
Carry flag = clear

If function unsuccessful
Carry flag = set
AH   = status
                86H   *if cassette not present*

Note:

- This function is available only on the PC and the PCjr. It is not supported on the PC/XT and all subsequent models.

Int 15H Function 01H [PC]
Turn Off Cassette Motor

Turns off the motor of the cassette tape drive.

Call with:

AH   = 01H

Returns:

If function successful
Carry flag = clear

If function unsuccessful
Carry flag = set
AH   = status
                86H   *if cassette not present*

Note:

- This function is available only on the PC and the PCjr. It is not supported on the PC/XT and all subsequent models.

Int 15H Function 02H [PC]
Read Cassette

Reads one or more 256-byte blocks of data from the cassette tape drive to memory.

Call with:

AH   = 02H
CX   = number of bytes to read
ES:BX   = segment:offset of buffer

Returns:

If function successful
Carry flag = clear
DX   = number of bytes actually read
ES:BX   = segment:offset + 1 of last byte read

If function unsuccessful
Carry flag = set
AH   = status
            01H   if CRC error
            02H   if bit signals scrambled
            04H   if no data found
            80H   if invalid command
            86H   if cassette not present

Note:

■ This function is available only on the PC and the PCjr. It is not supported on the PC/XT and all subsequent models.

Int 15H Function 03H   [PC]
Write Cassette

Writes one or more 256-byte blocks of data from memory to the cassette tape drive.

Call with:

AH   = 03H
CX   = number of bytes to write
ES:BX   = segment:offset of buffer

Returns:

If function successful
Carry flag = clear
CX   = 00H
ES:BX   = segment:offset + 1 of last byte written

If function unsuccessful
Carry flag = set
AH = status
       80H   if invalid command
       86H   if cassette not present

Note:

- This function is available only on the PC and the PCjr. It is not supported on the PC/XT and all subsequent models.

Int 15H Function 0FH   [PS/2]
Format ESDI Drive Periodic Interrupt

Invoked by the ROM BIOS on the ESDI Fixed Disk Drive Adapter/A during a format or surface analysis operation after each cylinder is completed.

Call with:

AH = 0FH
AL = phase code
      0 = reserved
      1 = surface analysis
      2 = formatting

Returns:

If formatting or analysis should continue
Carry flag = clear

If formatting or analysis should be terminated
Carry flag = set

Notes:

- This function call can be captured by a program so that it will be notified as each cylinder is formatted or analyzed. The program can count interrupts for each phase to determine the current cylinder number.

- The ROM BIOS default handler for this function returns with the carry flag set.

Int 15H Function 21H
Subfunction 00H
Read POST Error Log

[PS/2]

Returns error information that was accumulated during the most recent power-on self-test (POST).

Call with:

AH = 21H
AL = 00H

Returns:

If function successful
Carry flag = clear
AH   = 00H
BX   = number of POST error codes stored
ES:DI = segment:offset of POST error log

If function unsuccessful
Carry flag = set
AH   = status
    80H = invalid command
    86H = function not supported

Notes:

- The error log consists of single-word entries. The first byte of an entry is the device error code; the second is the device identifier.

- This function is not available on the PS/2 Models 25 and 30.

Int 15H Function 21H
Subfunction 01H
Write POST Error Log

[PS/2]

Adds an entry to the power-on self-test (POST) error log.

Call with:

AH = 21H
AL = 01H
BH = device identifier
BL = device error code

Returns:

If function successful
Carry flag = clear
AH   = 00H

If function unsuccessful
Carry flag = set
AH   = status
      01H = *error list full*
      80H = *invalid command*
      86H = *function not supported*

Note:

▪ This function is not available on the PS/2 Models 25 and 30.

Int 15H Function 4FH   [PS/2]
Keyboard Intercept

Invoked for each keystroke by the ROM BIOS's Int 09H keyboard interrupt handler.

Call with:

AH   = 4FH
AL   = scan code

Returns:

If scan code consumed
Carry flag = clear

If scan code not consumed
Carry flag = set
AL   = unchanged or new scan code

Notes:

▪ An operating system or a resident utility can capture this function to filter the raw keyboard data stream. The new handler can substitute a new scan code, return the same scan code, or return the carry flag clear causing the keystroke to be discarded. The ROM BIOS default routine simply returns the scan code unchanged.

▪ A program can call Int 15H Function C0H to determine whether the host machine's ROM BIOS supports this keyboard intercept.

Int 15H Function 80H
Device Open

Acquires ownership of a logical device for a process.

Call with:

AH	= 80H
BX	= device ID
CX	= process ID

Returns:

If function successful
Carry flag = clear
AH = 00H

If function unsuccessful
Carry flag = set
AH = status

Note:

■ This function call, along with Int 15H Functions 81H and 82H, defines a simple protocol that can be used to arbitrate usage of devices by multiple processes. A multitasking program manager would be expected to capture Int 15H and provide the appropriate service. The default BIOS routine for this function simply returns with the carry flag clear and AH = 00H.

Int 15H Function 81H
Device Close

Releases ownership of a logical device for a process.

Call with:

AH	= 81H
BX	= device ID
CX	= process ID

Returns:

If function successful
Carry flag = clear
AH   = 00H

If function unsuccessful
Carry flag = set
AH   = status

Note:

- A multitasking program manager would be expected to capture Int 15H and provide the appropriate service. The ROM BIOS default routine for this function simply returns with the carry flag clear and AH = 00H. See also Int 15H Functions 80H and 82H.

Int 15H Function 82H [AT] [PS/2]
Process Termination

Releases ownership of all logical devices for a process that is about to terminate.

Call with:

AH   = 82H
BX   = process ID

Returns:

If function successful
Carry flag = clear
AH   = 00H

If function unsuccessful
Carry flag = set
AH   = status

Note:

- A multitasking program manager would be expected to capture Int 15H and provide the appropriate service. The ROM BIOS default routine for this function simply returns with the carry flag clear and AH = 00H. See also Int 15H Functions 80H and 81H.

Int 15H Function 83H
Event Wait

[AT] [PS/2]

Requests setting of a semaphore after a specified interval or cancels a previous request.

Call with:

If requesting event wait
AH   = 83H
AL   = 00H
CX:DX   = microseconds
ES:BX   = segment:offset of semaphore byte

If canceling event wait
AH   = 83H
AL   = 01H

Returns:

If called with AL = 00H, and function successful
Carry flag   = clear

If called with AL = 00H, and function unsuccessful (Event Wait already active)
Carry flag   = set

If called with AL = 01H
Nothing

Notes:

■ The function call returns immediately. If the function is successful, bit 7 of the semaphore byte is set when the specified interval has elapsed. The calling program is responsible for clearing the semaphore before requesting this function.

■ The actual duration of an event wait is always an integral multiple of 976 microseconds. The CMOS date/clock chip interrupts are used to implement this function.

■ Use of this function allows programmed, hardware-independent delays at a finer resolution than can be obtained through use of the MS-DOS Get Time function (Int 21H Function 2CH, which returns time in hundredths of a second).

■ See also Int 15H Function 86H, which suspends the calling program for the specified interval in milliseconds.

■ This function is not supported on the PS/2 Models 25 and 30.

Int 15H Function 84H [AT] [PS/2]
Read Joystick

Returns the joystick switch settings and potentiometer values.

Call with:

AH   = 84H
DX   = subfunction
         00H   to read switch settings
         01H   to read resistive inputs

Returns:

If function successful
Carry flag = clear

and, if called with DX = 00H
AL   = switch settings (bits 4−7)

or, if called with DX = 01H
AX   = A(x) value
BX   = A(y) value
CX   = B(x) value
DX   = B(y) value

If function unsuccessful
Carry flag = set

Notes:

- An error condition is returned if DX does not contain a valid subfunction number.

- If no game adapter is installed, AL is returned as 00H for Subfunction 00H (i.e., all switches open); AX, BX, CX, and DX are returned containing 00H for Subfunction 01H.

- Using a 250 KOhm joystick, the potentiometer values usually lie within the range 0−416 (0000−01A0H).

Int 15H Function 85H [AT] [PS/2]
SysReq Key

Invoked by the ROM BIOS keyboard driver when the SysReq key is detected.

Call with:

AH   = 85H
AL   = key status
                00H   if key make (depression)
                01H   if key break (release)

Returns:

If function successful
Carry flag = clear
AH   = 00H

If function unsuccessful
Carry flag = set
AH   = status

Note:

- The ROM BIOS handler for this function call is a dummy routine that always returns a success status unless called with an invalid subfunction number in AL. A multitasking program manager would be expected to capture Int 15H so that it can be notified when the user strikes the SysReq key.

Int 15H Function 86H   [AT] [PS/2]
Delay

Suspends the calling program for a specified interval in microseconds.

Call with:

AH   = 86H
CX:DX   = microseconds to wait

Returns:

If function successful (wait was performed)
Carry flag = clear

If function unsuccessful (wait was not performed)
Carry flag = set

Notes:

- The actual duration of the wait is always an integral multiple of 976 microseconds.

- Use of this function allows programmed, hardware-independent delays at a finer resolution than can be obtained through use of the MS-DOS Get Time function (Int 21H Function 2CH, which returns time in hundredths of a second).

- See also Int 15H Function 83H, which triggers a semaphore after a specified interval but does not suspend the calling program.

Int 15H Function 87H [AT] [PS/2]
Move Extended Memory Block

Transfers data between conventional memory and extended memory.

Call with:

AH	= 87H
CX	= number of words to move
ES:SI	= segment:offset of Global Descriptor Table (see Notes)

Returns:

If function successful
Carry flag = clear
AH = 00H

If function unsuccessful
Carry flag = set
AH = status

01H	*if RAM parity error*
02H	*if exception interrupt error*
03H	*if gate address line 20 failed*

Notes:

- Conventional memory lies at addresses below the 640 KB boundary, and is used for the execution of MS-DOS and its application programs. Extended memory lies at addresses above 1 MB, and can only be accessed by an 80286 or 80386 CPU running in protected mode. As much as 15 MB of extended memory can be installed in a PC/AT or compatible.

- The Global Descriptor Table (GDT) used by this function must be set up as follows:

Byte(s)	Contents
00H–0FH	reserved (should be 0)
10H–11H	segment length in bytes (2∗CX − 1 or greater)
12H–14H	24-bit source address
15H	access rights byte (always 93H)
16H–17H	reserved (should be 0)
18H–19H	segment length in bytes (2∗CX − 1 or greater)
1AH–1CH	24-bit destination address
1DH	access rights byte (always 93H)
1EH–2FH	reserved (should be 0)

The table is composed of six 8-byte descriptors to be used by the CPU in protected mode. The four descriptors in offsets 00H–0FH and 20H–2FH are filled in by the ROM BIOS before the CPU mode switch.

- The addresses used in the descriptor table are linear (physical) 24-bit addresses in the range 000000H–FFFFFFH—not segments and offsets—with the least significant byte at the lowest address and the most significant byte at the highest address.

- The block move is performed with interrupts disabled; thus, use of this function may interfere with the operation of communications programs, network drivers, or other software that relies on prompt servicing of hardware interrupts.

- Programs and drivers that access extended memory with this function cannot be executed in the Compatibility Environment of OS/2.

- This function is not supported on the PS/2 Models 25 and 30.

Int 15H Function 88H [AT] [PS/2]
Get Extended Memory Size

Returns the amount of extended memory installed in the system.

Call with:

    AH   = 88H

Returns:

    AX   = amount of extended memory (in KB)

Notes:

- Extended memory is memory at addresses above 1 MB, which can only be accessed by an 80286 or 80386 CPU running in protected mode. Because MS-DOS is a real-mode operating system, extended memory can be used for storage of volatile data but cannot be used for execution of programs.

- Programs and drivers that use this function cannot be executed in the Compatibility Environment of OS/2.

- This function is not supported on the PS/2 Models 25 and 30.

Int 15H Function 89H [AT] [PS/2]
Enter Protected Mode

Switches the CPU from real mode into protected mode.

Call with:

AH	= 89H
BH	= interrupt number for IRQ0, written to ICW2 of 8259 PIC #1 (must be evenly divisible by 8, determines IRQ0–IRQ7)
BL	= interrupt number for IRQ8, written to ICW2 of 8259 PIC #2 (must be evenly divisible by 8, determines IRQ8–IRQ15)
ES:SI	= segment:offset of Global Descriptor Table (GDT)

Returns:

If function successful (CPU is in protected mode)

Carry flag	= clear
AH	= 00H
CS	= user-defined selector
DS	= user-defined selector
ES	= user-defined selector
SS	= user-defined selector

If function unsuccessful (CPU is in real mode)

Carry flag	= set
AH	= FFH

Notes:

- The Global Descriptor Table must contain eight descriptors set up as follows:

Offset	Descriptor usage
00H	dummy descriptor (initialized to 0)
08H	Global Descriptor Table (GDT)
10H	Interrupt Descriptor Table (IDT)
18H	user's data segment (DS)
20H	user's extra segment (ES)
28H	user's stack segment (SS)
30H	user's code segment (CS)
38H	BIOS code segment

The user must initialize the first seven descriptors; the eighth is filled in by the ROM BIOS to provide addressability for its own execution. The calling program may modify and use the eighth descriptor for any purpose after return from this function call.

- This function is not supported on the PS/2 Models 25 and 30.

Int 15H Function 90H
Device Wait

[AT] [PS/2]

Invoked by the ROM BIOS fixed disk, floppy disk, printer, network, and keyboard drivers prior to performing a programmed wait for I/O completion.

Call with:

AH	= 90H
AL	= device type
	00H–7FH *serially reusable devices*
	80H–BFH *reentrant devices*
	C0H–FFH *wait-only calls, no corresponding Post function*
ES:BX	= segment:offset of request block for device types 80H–FFH

Returns:

If no wait (driver must perform its own time-out)
Carry flag = clear
AH   = 00H

If wait was performed
Carry flag = set

Notes:

■ Predefined device types are:

00H	disk (may time-out)
01H	floppy disk (may time-out)
02H	keyboard (no time-out)
03H	pointing device (PS/2, may time-out)
80H	network (no time-out)
FCH	fixed disk reset (PS/2, may time-out)
FDH	floppy disk drive motor start (may time-out)
FEH	printer (may time-out)

■ For network adapters, ES:BX points to a network control block (NCB).

■ A multitasking program manager would be expected to capture Int 15H Function 90H so that it can dispatch other tasks while I/O is in progress. The default BIOS routine for this function simply returns with the carry flag clear and AH = 00H.

Int 15H Function 91H   [AT] [PS/2]
Device Post

Invoked by the ROM BIOS fixed disk, floppy disk, network, and keyboard drivers to signal that I/O is complete and/or the device is ready.

Call with:

AH	= 91H
AL	= device type
	00H–7FH serially reusable devices
	80H–BFH reentrant devices
ES:BX	= segment:offset of request block for device types 80H–BFH

Returns:

AH   = 00H

Notes:

■ Predefined device types that may use Device Post are:

00H	disk (may time-out)
01H	floppy disk (may time-out)
02H	keyboard (no time-out)
03H	pointing device (PS/2, may time-out)
80H	network (no time-out)

■ The ROM BIOS printer routine does not invoke this function because printer output is not interrupt driven.

■ A multitasking program manager would be expected to capture Int 15H Function 91H so that it can be notified when I/O is completed and awaken the requesting task. The default BIOS routine for this function simply returns with the carry flag clear and AH = 00H.

Int 15H Function C0H   [AT] [PS/2]
Get System Environment

Returns a pointer to a table containing various information about the system configuration.

Call with:

AH   = C0H

Returns:

ES:BX   = segment:offset of configuration table (see Notes)

Notes:

■ The format of the system configuration table is as follows:

Byte(s)	Contents
00H–01H	length of table in bytes
02H	system model (see following Note)
03H	system submodel (see following Note)
04H	BIOS revision level

(continued)

Byte(s)	Contents
05H	configuration flags

Bit	Significance (if set)
7	DMA channel 3 used
6	slave 8259 present (cascaded IRQ2)
5	real-time clock available
4	keyboard intercept (Int 15H Function 4FH) available
3	Wait for External Event is available
2	extended BIOS data area allocated
1	Micro Channel implemented
0	reserved

Byte(s)	Contents
06H–09H	reserved

■ The system model and type bytes are assigned as follows:

Machine	Model Byte	Submodel Byte
PC	FFH	
PC/XT	FEH	
PC/XT	FBH	00H or 01H
PCjr	FDH	
PC/AT	FCH	00H or 01H
PC/XT-286	FCH	02H
PC Convertible	F9H	
PS/2 Model 30	FAH	00H
PS/2 Model 50	FCH	04H
PS/2 Model 60	FCH	05H
PS/2 Model 80	F8H	00H or 01H

Int 15H Function C1H   [PS/2]
Get Address of Extended BIOS Data Area

Returns the segment address of the base of the extended BIOS data area.

Call with:

AH   = C1H

Returns:

If function successful
Carry flag = clear
ES   = segment of extended BIOS data area

If function unsuccessful
Carry flag = set

Notes:

■ The extended BIOS data area is allocated at the high end of
conventional memory during the POST (Power-On-Self-Test)
sequence. The word at 0040:0013H (memory size) is updated to
reflect the reduced amount of memory available for MS-DOS and
application programs. The first byte in the extended BIOS data
area is initialized to its length in KB.

■ A program can determine whether the extended BIOS data area
exists with Int 15H Function C0H.

Int 15H Function C2H   [PS/2]
Subfunction 00H
Enable/Disable Pointing Device

Enables or disables the system's mouse or other pointing device.

Call with:

AH   = C2H
AL   = 00H
BH   = enable/disable flag
          00H   = disable
          01H   = enable

Returns:

If function successful
Carry flag = clear
AH   = 00H

If function unsuccessful
Carry flag = set
AH   = status
              01H   if invalid function call
              02H   if invalid input
              03H   if interface error
              04H   if resend
              05H   if no far call installed

Int 15H Function C2H
Subfunction 01H
Reset Pointing Device

[PS/2]

Resets the system's mouse or other pointing device, setting the sample rate, resolution, and other characteristics to their default values.

Call with:

AH = C2H
AL = 01H

Returns:

If function successful
Carry flag = clear
AH = 00H
BH = device ID

If function unsuccessful
Carry flag = set
AH = status (see Int 15H Function C2H Subfunction 00H)

Notes:

■ After a reset operation, the state of the pointing device is as follows:

disabled;
sample rate at 100 reports per second;
resolution at 4 counts per millimeter;
and scaling at 1 to 1.

The data package size is unchanged by this function.

■ The application can use the other Int 15H Function C2H subfunctions to initialize the pointing device to other sample rates, resolution, and scaling, and then enable the device with Int 15H Function C2H Subfunction 00H.

■ See also Int 15H Function C2H Subfunction 05H, which incidentally resets the pointing device in a similar manner.

Int 15H Function C2H [PS/2]
Subfunction 02H
Set Sample Rate

Sets the sampling rate of the system's mouse or other pointing device.

Call with:

AH	= C2H
AL	= 02H
BH	= sample rate value

00H	*= 10 reports per second*
01H	*= 20 reports per second*
02H	*= 40 reports per second*
03H	*= 60 reports per second*
04H	*= 80 reports per second*
05H	*= 100 reports per second*
06H	*= 200 reports per second*

Returns:

If function successful
Carry flag = clear
AH = 00H

If function unsuccessful
Carry flag = set
AH = status (see Int 15H Function C2H Subfunction 00H)

Note:

■ The default sample rate is 100 reports per second after a reset operation (Int 15H Function C2H Subfunction 01H).

Int 15H Function C2H [PS/2]
Subfunction 03H
Set Resolution

Sets the resolution of the system's mouse or other pointing device.

Call with:

AH = C2H
AL = 03H
BH = resolution value
      00H = 1 count per millimeter
      01H = 2 counts per millimeter
      02H = 4 counts per millimeter
      03H = 8 counts per millimeter

Returns:

If function successful
Carry flag = clear
AH = 00H

If function unsuccessful
Carry flag = set
AH = status (see Int 15H Function C2H Subfunction 00H)

Note:

■ The default resolution is 4 counts per millimeter after a reset operation (Int 15H Function C2H Subfunction 01H).

Int 15H Function C2H [PS/2]
Subfunction 04H
Get Pointing Device Type

Returns the identification code for the system's mouse or other pointing device.

Call with:

AH = C2H
AL = 04H

Returns:

If function successful
Carry flag = clear
AH = 00H
BH = device ID

If function unsuccessful
Carry flag = set
AH = status (see Int 15H Function C2H Subfunction 00H)

Int 15H Function C2H [PS/2]
Subfunction 05H
Initialize Pointing Device Interface

Sets the data package size for the system's mouse or other pointing device, and initializes the resolution, sampling rate, and scaling to their default values.

Call with:

AH	= C2H
AL	= 05H
BH	= data package size in bytes (1–8)

Returns:

If function successful
Carry flag = clear
AH = 00H

If function unsuccessful
Carry flag = set
AH = status (see Int 15H Function C2H Subfunction 00H)

Note:

■ After this operation, the state of the pointing device is as follows:

disabled;
sample rate at 100 reports per second;
resolution at 4 counts per millimeter;
and scaling at 1 to 1.

Int 15H Function C2H [PS/2]
Subfunction 06H
Set Scaling or Get Status

Returns the current status of the system's mouse or other pointing device or sets the device's scaling factor.

Call with:

AH = C2H
AL = 06H
BH = extended command
    00H = *return device status*
    01H = *set scaling at 1:1*
    02H = *set scaling at 2:1*

Returns:

If function successful
Carry flag = clear
AH = 00H

and, if called with BH = 00H
BL = status byte

Bit	Significance
0	*= 1 if right button pressed*
1	*= reserved*
2	*= 1 if left button pressed*
3	*= reserved*
4	*= 0 if 1:1 scaling*
	1 if 2:1 scaling
5	*= 0 if device disabled*
	1 if device enabled
6	*= 0 if stream mode*
	1 if remote mode
7	*= reserved*

CL = resolution
    00H = *1 count per millimeter*
    01H = *2 counts per millimeter*
    02H = *4 counts per millimeter*
    03H = *8 counts per millimeter*
DL = sample rate
    0AH = *10 reports per second*
    14H = *20 reports per second*
    28H = *40 reports per second*
    3CH = *60 reports per second*
    50H = *80 reports per second*
    64H = *100 reports per second*
    C8H = *200 reports per second*

If function unsuccessful
Carry flag = set
AH = status (see Int 15H Function C2H Subfunction 00H)

Int 15H Function C2H
Subfunction 07H
Set Pointing Device Handler Address

[PS/2]

Notifies the ROM BIOS pointing device driver of the address for a routine to be called each time pointing device data is available.

Call with:

AH	= C2H
AL	= 07H
ES:BX	= segment:offset of user routine

Returns:

If function successful
Carry flag = clear

If function unsuccessful
Carry flag = set
AH = status (see Int 15H Function C2H Subfunction 00H)

Notes:

■ The user's handler for pointing device data is entered via a far call with four parameters on the stack:

SS:SP+0AH	status
SS:SP+08H	x coordinate
SS:SP+06H	y coordinate
SS:SP+04H	z coordinate (always 0)

The handler must exit via a far return without removing the parameters from the stack.

■ The status parameter passed to the user's handler is interpreted as follows:

Bit(s)	*Significance (if set)*
0	left button pressed
1	right button pressed
2–3	reserved
4	sign of x data is negative
5	sign of y data is negative
6	x data has overflowed
7	y data has overflowed
8–15	reserved

Int 15H Function C3H
Set Watchdog Time-Out

Enables or disables a watchdog timer.

Call with:

AH	= C3H
AL	= subfunction
	00H *to disable watchdog time-out*
	01H *to enable watchdog time-out*
BX	= watchdog timer counter (if AL = 01H)

Returns:

If function successful
Carry flag = clear

If function unsuccessful
Carry flag = set

Notes:

■ The watchdog timer generates an NMI interrupt.

■ This function is not available on the PS/2 Models 25 and 30.

Int 15H Function C4H
Programmable Option Select

Returns the base Programmable Option Select register address, enables a slot for setup, or enables an adapter.

Call with:

AH	= C4H
AL	= subfunction
	00H *to return base POS adapter register address*
	01H *to enable slot*
	02H *to enable adapter*
BL	= slot number (if AL = 01H)

Returns:

If function successful
Carry flag = clear

and, if called with AL = 00H
DX   = base POS adapter register address

If function unsuccessful
Carry flag = set

Notes:

- This function is available only on machines using the Micro Channel Architecture (MCA) bus.

- After a slot is enabled with Subfunction 01H, specific information can be obtained for the adapter in that slot by performing port input operations:

Port	Function
100H	MCA ID (low byte)
101H	MCA ID (high byte)
102H	Option Select Byte 1
	bit 0 = 1 if enabled, = 0 if disabled
103H	Option Select Byte 2
104H	Option Select Byte 3
105H	Option Select Byte 4
	bits 6–7 = channel check indicators
106H	Subaddress Extension (low byte)
107H	Subaddress Extension (high byte)

Int 16H Function 00H   [PC] [AT] [PS/2]
Read Character from Keyboard

Reads a character from the keyboard, also returning the keyboard scan code.

Call with:

AH   = 00H

Returns:

AH   = keyboard scan code
AL   = ASCII character

Int 16H Function 01H
Get Keyboard Status

Determines whether a character is ready for input, returning a flag
and also the character itself, if one is waiting.

Call with:

AH   = 01H

Returns:

If key waiting to be input
Zero flag   = clear
AH   = keyboard scan code
AL   = character

If no key waiting
Zero flag   = set

Note:

■ The character returned by this function when the zero flag is clear
is not removed from the type-ahead buffer. The same character and
scan code will be returned by the next call to Int 16H Function
00H.

Int 16H Function 02H
Get Keyboard Flags

Returns the ROM BIOS flags byte that describes the state of the
various keyboard toggles and shift keys.

Call with:

AH   = 02H

Returns:

AL   = flags

Bit	Significance (if set)
7	Insert on
6	Caps Lock on
5	Num Lock on

(continued)

Bit	Significance (if set)
4	Scroll Lock on
3	Alt key is down
2	Ctrl key is down
1	left Shift key is down
0	right Shift key is down

Note:

■ The keyboard flags byte is stored in the ROM BIOS data area at 0000:0417H.

Int 16H Function 03H   [PC] [AT] [PS/2]
Set Repeat Rate

Sets the ROM BIOS key repeat ("typematic") rate and delay.

Call with:

On the PC/AT and PS/2

AH	= 03H
AL	= 05H
BH	= repeat delay (see Notes)
BL	= repeat rate (see Notes)

On the PCjr

AH	= 03H
AL	= subfunction

     00H   *to restore default rate and delay*

     01H   *to increase initial delay*

     02H   *to decrease repeat rate by one-half*

     03H   *to increase delay and decrease repeat rate by one-half*

     04H   *to turn off keyboard repeat*

Returns:

Nothing

Notes:

■ Subfunctions 00H–04H are available on the PCjr but are not supported by the PC or PC/XT ROM BIOS. Subfunction 05H is available on PC/ATs with ROM BIOS's dated 11/15/85 and later, and on the PS/2.

- On the PC/AT and PS/2, the value in BH controls the amount of delay before the first repeat key is generated, and is a multiple of 250 milliseconds:

Value	Delay (msec.)
00H	250
01H	500
02H	750
03H	1000

- On the PC/AT and PS/2, the value for the repeat rate in characters per second can be chosen from the following table:

Value	Repeat rate (characters per second)
00H	30.0
01H	26.7
02H	24.0
03H	21.8
04H	20.0
05H	18.5
06H	17.1
07H	16.0
08H	15.0
09H	13.3
0AH	12.0
0BH	10.9
0CH	10.0
0DH	9.2
0EH	8.6
0FH	8.0
10H	7.5
11H	6.7
12H	6.0
13H	5.5
14H	5.0
15H	4.6
16H	4.3

(continued)

Value	Repeat rate (characters per second)
17H	4.0
18H	3.7
19H	3.3
1AH	3.0
1BH	2.7
1CH	2.5
1DH	2.3
1EH	2.1
1FH	2.0

Int 16H Function 04H [PC]
Set Keyclick

Turns the keyboard click on or off.

Call with:

AH = 04H
AL = subfunction
    00H to turn off keyboard click
    01H to turn on keyboard click

Returns:

Nothing

Note:

■ This function is supported by the PCjr BIOS only.

Int 16H Function 05H [AT] [PS/2]
Push Character and Scan Code

Places a character and scan code in the keyboard type-ahead buffer.

Call with:

AH = 05H
CH = scan code
CL = character

Returns:

If function successful
Carry flag = clear
AL   = 00H

If function unsuccessful (type-ahead buffer is full)
Carry flag = set
AL   = 01H

Note:

■ This function can be used by keyboard enhancers and other utilities to interpolate keys into the data stream seen by application programs.

Int 16H Function 10H   [AT] [PS/2]
Read Character from
Enhanced Keyboard

Reads a character and scan code from the keyboard type-ahead buffer.

Call with:

AH   = 10H

Returns:

AH   = keyboard scan code
AL   = ASCII character

Note:

■ Use this function for the enhanced keyboard instead of Int 16H Function 00H. It allows applications to obtain the scan codes for the additional F11, F12, and cursor control keys.

Int 16H Function 11H   [AT] [PS/2]
Get Enhanced Keyboard Status

Determines whether a character is ready for input, returning a flag and also the character itself, if one is waiting.

Call with:

AH   = 11H

Returns:

If key waiting to be input
Zero flag = clear
AH   = keyboard scan code
AL   = character

If no key waiting
Zero flag = set

Notes:

- Use this function for the enhanced keyboard instead of Int 16H Function 00H. It allows applications to test for the additional F11, F12, and cursor control keys.

- The character returned by this function when the zero flag is clear is not removed from the type-ahead buffer. The same character and scan code will be returned by the next call to Int 16H Function 10H.

Int 16H Function 12H [AT] [PS/2]
Get Enhanced Keyboard Flags

Obtains the status of various enhanced keyboard special keys and keyboard driver states.

Call with:

AH   = 12H

Returns:

AX   = flags

Bit	Significance (if set)
00H	*right Shift key is down*
01H	*left Shift key is down*
02H	*either Ctrl key is down*
03H	*either Alt key is down*
04H	*Scroll Lock toggle is on*
05H	*Num Lock toggle is on*
06H	*Caps Lock toggle is on*
07H	*Insert toggle is on*
08H	*left Ctrl key is down*
09H	*left Alt key is down*

(continued)

Bit	Significance (if set)
0AH	right Ctrl key is down
0BH	right Alt key is down
0CH	Scroll key is down
0DH	Num Lock key is down
0EH	Caps Lock key is down
0FH	SysReq key is down

Note:

- Use this function for the enhanced keyboard instead of Int 16H Function 02H.

Int 17H Function 00H [PC] [AT]
Write Character to Printer

Sends a character to the specified parallel printer interface port and returns the current status of the port.

Call with:

AH	= 00H
AL	= character
DX	= printer number (0 = LPT1, 1 = LPT2, 2 = LPT3)

Returns:

AH = status

Bit	Significance (if set)
7	printer not busy
6	printer acknowledge
5	out of paper
4	printer selected
3	I/O error
2	unused
1	unused
0	printer timed-out

Int 17H Function 01H [PC] [AT] [PS/2]
Initialize Printer Port

Initializes the specified parallel printer interface port, and returns its status.

Int 17H Function 02H   [PC] [AT] [PS/2]
Get Printer Status

Returns the current status of the specified parallel printer interface port.

Call with:

AH   = 02H
DX   = printer number (0 = LPT1, 1 = LPT2, 2 = LPT3)

Returns:

AH   = status (see Int 17H Function 00H)

Int 18H   [PC] [AT] [PS/2]
ROM BASIC

Transfers control to ROM BASIC.

Call with:

Nothing

Returns:

Nothing

Note:

■ This function is invoked when the system is turned on or restarted if attempts to read a boot sector from the fixed disk or floppy disk drives are unsuccessful.

Int 19H
Reboot System

Reboots the operating system from the floppy disk or fixed disk drive.

Call with:

Nothing

Returns:

Nothing

Notes:

- The bootstrap routine reads Sector 1, Track 0 into memory at location 0000:7C00H and transfers control to the same address. If attempts to read a boot sector from the floppy disk or fixed disk are unsuccessful, control is transferred to ROM BASIC by execution of an Int 18H.

- If location 0000:0472H does not contain the value 1234H, a memory test will be performed before reading the boot sector.

Int 1AH Function 00H
Get Tick Count

Returns the contents of the clock tick counter.

Call with:

AH	= 00H

Returns:

AL	= rolled-over flag	
	00H	*if midnight not passed since last read*
	<>00H	*if midnight was passed since last read*
CX:DX	= tick count (high 16 bits in CX)	

Notes:

- This function is supported by the PC/XT and PCjr ROM BIOS, but is not present in the ROM BIOS for the original PC.

- The returned value is the cumulative number of clock ticks since midnight. There are 18.2 clock ticks per second. When the counter reaches 1,573,040, it is cleared to zero, and the rolled-over flag is set.

- The rolled-over flag is cleared by this function call, so the flag will only be returned nonzero once per day.

- Int 1AH Function 01H can be used to set the clock tick counter to an arbitrary 32-bit value.

Int 1AH Function 01H
Set Tick Count

[AT] [PS/2]

Stores a 32-bit value in the clock tick counter.

Call with:

AH	= 01H
CX:DX	= tick count (high 16-bits in CX)

Returns:

Nothing

Notes:

- This function is supported by the PC/XT and PCjr ROM BIOS, but is not present in the ROM BIOS for the original PC.

- Int 1AH Function 00H is used to read the value of the clock tick counter.

- The rolled-over flag is cleared by this function call.

Int 1AH Function 02H
Get Time

[AT] [PS/2]

Reads the current time from the CMOS time/date chip.

Call with:

AH	= 02H

Returns:

CH	= hours in binary coded decimal (BCD)
CL	= minutes in BCD

DH	= seconds in BCD
DL	= daylight-saving-time code
	00H *if standard time*
	01H *if daylight saving time*

and, if clock running
Carry flag = clear

or, if clock stopped
Carry flag = set

Int 1AH Function 03H   [AT] [PS/2]
Set Time

Sets the time in the CMOS time/date chip.

Call with:

AHM	= 03H
CH	= hours in binary coded decimal (BCD)
CL	= minutes in BCD
DH	= seconds in BCD
DL	= daylight-saving-time code
	00H *if standard time*
	01H *if daylight saving time*

Returns:

Nothing

Int 1AH Function 04H   [AT] [PS/2]
Get Date

Reads the current date from the CMOS time/date chip.

Call with:

| AH | = 04H |

Returns:

CH	= century (19 or 20) in binary coded decimal (BCD)
CL	= year in BCD
DH	= month in BCD
DL	= day in BCD

and, if clock running
Carry flag = clear

or, if clock stopped
Carry flag = set

Int 1AH Function 05H [AT] [PS/2]
Set Date

Sets the date in the CMOS time/date chip.

Call with:

AH	= 05H
CH	= century (19 or 20) in binary coded decimal (BCD)
CL	= year in BCD
DH	= month in BCD
DL	= day in BCD

Returns:

Nothing

Int 1AH Function 06H [AT] [PS/2]
Set Alarm

Sets an alarm in the CMOS date/time chip.

Call with:

AH	= 06H
CH	= hours in binary coded decimal (BCD)
CL	= minutes in BCD
DH	= seconds in BCD

Returns:

If function successful
Carry flag = clear

If function unsuccessful (alarm already set, or clock stopped)
Carry flag = set

Notes:

- A side effect of this function is that the clock chip's interrupt level (IRQ8) is enabled.

- Only one alarm may be active at any given time. The alarm occurs every 24 hours at the specified time until it is reset with Int 1AH Function 07H.

- The program using this function must place the address of its interrupt handler for the alarm in the vector for Int 4AH.

Int 1AH Function 07H [AT] [PS/2]
Reset Alarm

Cancels any pending alarm request on the CMOS date/time chip.

Call with:

AH   = 07H

Returns:

Nothing

Note:

- This function does not disable the clock chip's interrupt level (IRQ8).

Int 1AH Function 0AH [PS/2]
Get Day Count

Returns the contents of the system's day counter.

Call with:

AH   = 0AH

Returns:

If function successful
Carry flag = clear
CX   = count of days since 1-1-1980

If function unsuccessful
Carry flag = set

Int 1AH Function 0BH
Set Day Count

Stores an arbitrary value in the system's day counter.

Call with:

AH	= 0BH
CX	= count of days since January 1, 1980

Returns:

If function successful
Carry flag = clear

If function unsuccessful
Carry flag = set

Int 1AH Function 80H
Set Sound Source

Sets up the source for tones that will appear on the PCjr's "Audio Out" or RF modulator.

Call with:

AH	= 80H
AL	= sound source

    00H   if 8253 programmable timer, channel 2
    01H   if cassette input
    02H   if "Audio In" line on I/O channel
    03H   if sound generator chip

Returns:

Nothing

Note:

■ This function is supported on the PCjr only.

Interrupt Usage

Interrupt	Used for	Model
00H	Divide by zero	PC, AT, PS/2
01H	Single step	PC, AT, PS/2
02H	NMI	PC, AT, PS/2
03H	Breakpoint	PC, AT, PS/2
04H	Overflow	PC, AT, PS/2
05H	ROM BIOS PrintScreen	PC, AT, PS/2
	Bounds exception*	AT, PS/2
06H	Reserved	PC
	Invalid opcode*	AT, PS/2
07H	Reserved	PC
	80287/387 not present*	AT, PS/2
08H	IRQ0 timer tick	PC, AT, PS/2
	Double exception error*	AT, PS/2
09H	IRQ1 keyboard	PC, AT, PS/2
	80287/387 segment overrun*	AT, PS/2
0AH	IRQ2 reserved	PC
	IRQ2 cascade from slave 8259 PIC	AT, PS/2
	Invalid TSS*	AT, PS/2
0BH	IRQ3 serial communications (COM2)	PC, AT, PS/2
	Segment not present*	AT, PS/2
0CH	IRQ4 serial communications (COM1)	PC, AT, PS/2
	Stack segment overflow*	AT, PS/2
0DH	IRQ5 fixed disk	PC
	IRQ5 parallel printer (LPT2)	AT
	Reserved	PS/2
	General protection fault*	AT, PS/2
0EH	IRQ6 floppy disk	PC, AT, PS/2
	Page fault†	AT, PS/2
0FH	IRQ7 parallel printer (LPT1)	PC, AT, PS/2
10H	ROM BIOS video driver	PC, AT, PS/2
	Numeric coprocessor fault*	AT, PS/2

*80286 and 80386 processors only
†80386 processor only

(continued)

Interrupt	*Used for*	*Model*
11H	ROM BIOS equipment check	PC, AT, PS/2
12H	ROM BIOS conventional memory size	PC, AT, PS/2
13H	ROM BIOS disk driver	PC, AT, PS/2
14H	ROM BIOS communications driver	PC, AT, PS/2
15H	ROM BIOS cassette driver	PC
	ROM BIOS I/O system extensions	AT, PS/2
16H	ROM BIOS keyboard driver	PC, AT, PS/2
17H	ROM BIOS printer driver	PC, AT, PS/2
18H	ROM BASIC	PC, AT, PS/2
19H	ROM BIOS bootstrap	PC, AT, PS/2
1AH	ROM BIOS time of day	AT, PS/2
1BH	ROM BIOS Ctrl-break	PC, AT, PS/2
1CH	ROM BIOS timer tick	PC, AT, PS/2
1DH	ROM BIOS video parameter table	PC, AT, PS/2
1EH	ROM BIOS floppy disk parameters	PC, AT, PS/2
1FH	ROM BIOS font (characters 80H–FFH)	PC, AT, PS/2
20H	MS-DOS terminate process	
21H	MS-DOS function dispatcher	
22H	MS-DOS terminate address	
23H	MS-DOS Ctrl-C handler address	
24H	MS-DOS critical-error handler address	
25H	MS-DOS absolute disk read	
26H	MS-DOS absolute disk write	
27H	MS-DOS terminate and stay resident	
28H	MS-DOS idle interrupt	
29H	MS-DOS reserved	
2AH	MS-DOS network redirector	
2BH–2EH	MS-DOS reserved	
2FH	MS-DOS multiplex interrupt	
30H–3FH	MS-DOS reserved	
40H	ROM BIOS floppy disk driver (if fixed disk installed)	PC, AT, PS/2

(continued)

Interrupt	Used for	Model
41H	ROM BIOS fixed disk parameters	PC
	ROM BIOS fixed disk parameters (drive 0)	AT, PS/2
42H	ROM BIOS default video driver (if EGA installed)	PC, AT, PS/2
43H	EGA, MCGA, VGA character table	PC, AT, PS/2
44H	ROM BIOS font (characters 00–7FH)	PCjr
46H	ROM BIOS fixed disk parameters (drive 1)	AT, PS/2
4AH	ROM BIOS alarm handler	AT, PS/2
5AH	Cluster adapter	PC, AT
5BH	Used by cluster program	PC, AT
60H–66H	User interrupts	PC, AT, PS/2
67H	LIM EMS driver	PC, AT, PS/2
70H	IRQ8 CMOS real-time clock	AT, PS/2
71H	IRQ9 software diverted to IRQ2	AT, PS/2
72H	IRQ10 reserved	AT, PS/2
73H	IRQ11 reserved	AT, PS/2
74H	IRQ12 reserved	AT
	IRQ12 mouse	PS/2
75H	IRQ13 numeric coprocessor	AT, PS/2
76H	IRQ14 fixed disk controller	AT, PS/2
77H	IRQ15 reserved	AT, PS/2
80H–F0H	BASIC	PC, AT, PS/2
F1H–FFH	Not used	PC, AT, PS/2

I/O Port Usage

Range	Usage	Model
0000–000FH	DMA controller 8237A	PC
0000–001FH	DMA controller 1, 8237A	AT
0000–001FH	DMA controller 1, 8237A-compatible	PS/2

(continued)

Range	Usage	Model
0020–0021H	Interrupt controller 1, 8259A	PC, AT, PS/2
0040–0043H	Programmable timer 8253	PC
0040–005FH	Programmable timer 8254	AT
0040–0047H	Programmable timers	PS/2
0060–0063H	Keyboard controller 8255A	PC
0060–006FH	Keyboard controller 8042	AT
0060H	Keyboard controller, auxiliary device	PS/2
0061H	System control port B	PS/2
0064H	Keyboard controller, auxiliary device	PS/2
0070–007FH	CMOS real-time clock, NMI mask	AT
0070–0071H	CMOS real-time clock, NMI mask	PS/2
0074–0076H	Reserved	PS/2
0080–008FH	DMA page registers	PS/2
0080–009FH	DMA page registers, 74LS612	AT
0090H	Central arbitration control port	PS/2
0091H	Card selected feedback	PS/2
0092H	System control port A	PS/2
0093H	Reserved	PS/2
0094H	System board setup	PS/2
0096–0097H	POS, channel connector select	PS/2
00A0H	NMI mask register	PC
00A0–00A1H	Interrupt controller 2, 8259A	AT, PS/2
00C0–00DFH	DMA controller 2, 8237A-5	AT, PS/2
00F0–00FFH	Math coprocessor	AT, PS/2
0100–0107H	Programmable option select	PS/2
01F0–01F8H	Fixed disk	AT, PS/2
0200–020FH	Game controller	PC, AT
0210–0217H	Expansion unit	PC
0278–027FH	Parallel printer port 2	AT
0278–027BH	Parallel printer port 3	PS/2
02B0–02DFH	EGA (alternate)	PC, AT
02E1H	GPIB (adapter 0)	AT
02E2–02E3H	Data acquisition (adapter 0)	AT
02F8–02FFH	Serial communications (COM2)	PC, AT, PS/2
0300–031FH	Prototype card	PC, AT
0320–032FH	Fixed disk	PC

(continued)

Range	Usage	Model
0360–036FH	PC Network	AT
0378–037FH	Parallel printer port 1	PC, AT
0378–037BH	Parallel printer port 2	PS/2
0380–038CH	SDLC communications	PC, AT
0380–0389H	BSC communications (alternate)	PC
0390–0393H	Cluster (adapter 0)	PC, AT
03A0–03A9H	BSC communications (primary)	PC, AT
03B0–03BFH	Monochrome/parallel printer adapter	PC, AT
03B4–03B5H	Video subsystem	PS/2
03BAH	Video subsystem	PS/2
03BC–03BFH	Parallel printer port 1	PS/2
03C0–03CFH	EGA (primary)	PC, AT
03C0–03DAH	Video subsystem and DAC	PS/2
03D0–03DFH	CGA	PC, AT
03F0–03F7H	Floppy disk controller	PC, AT, PS/2
03F8–03FFH	Serial communications (COM1)	PC, AT, PS/2
06E2–06E3H	Data acquisition (adapter 1)	AT
0790–0793H	Cluster (adapter 1)	PC, AT
0AE2–0AE3H	Data acquisition (adapter 2)	AT
0B90–0B93H	Cluster (adapter 2)	PC, AT
0EE2–0EE3H	Data acquisition (adapter 3)	AT
1390–1393H	Cluster (adapter 3)	PC, AT
22E1H	GPIB (adapter 1)	
2390–2393H	Cluster (adapter 4)	PC, AT
42E1H	GPIB (adapter 2)	AT
62E1H	GPIB (adapter 3)	AT
82E1H	GPIB (adapter 4)	AT
A2E1H	GPIB (adapter 5)	AT
C2E1H	GPIB (adapter 6)	AT
E2E1H	GPIB (adapter 7)	AT

Video Attributes and Colors

Attribute Byte for Video Display Mode 7

7	6	5	4	3	2	1	0
B	background			I	foreground		

B = blink

I = intensity

Display	Background	Foreground
No display (black)	000	000
No display (white)*	111	111
Underline	000	001
Normal video	000	111
Reverse video	111	000

*VGA only

Attribute Byte for Video Display Modes 0–3

7	6	5	4	3	2	1	0
B	background			I	foreground		

B = blink *or* background intensity (default = blink)

I = foreground intensity *or* character select (default = intensity)

The following table of color values assumes default palette programming and that the B or I bit controls intensity:

Value	Color	Value	Color
0	Black	8	Gray
1	Blue	9	Light blue
2	Green	10	Light green
3	Cyan	11	Light cyan
4	Red	12	Light red
5	Magenta	13	Light magenta
6	Brown	14	Yellow
7	White	15	Intense white

The manuscript for this book was prepared and submitted to
Microsoft Press in electronic form. Text files were processed and
formatted using Microsoft Word.

Cover design by Ted Mader & Associates
Interior text design by Greg Hickman
Principal typography by Carol Luke

Text composition by Microsoft Press in Times Roman with display
in Times Roman Bold, using the Magna composition system and the
Linotronic 300 laser imagesetter.